Colonial Style

Colonial Style

CREATING CLASSIC INTERIORS
IN YOUR CAPE, COLONIAL,
OR SALTBOX HOME

TREENA CROCHET

The Taunton Press

The Taunton Press
Inspiration for hands-on living®

The Taunton Press, Inc., 63 South Main Street, PO Box 5506, Newtown, CT 06470-5506
e-mail: tp@taunton.com

Distributed by Publishers Group West

Editor: Erica Sanders-Foege
Jacket/cover design: Lori Wendin
Interior design and Layout: Susan Fazekas
Illustrator: Melanie Powell
Photographer: Randy O'Rourke, unless noted

LIBRARY OF CONGRESS CATALOGING-IN-PUBLICATION DATA
Crochet, Treena.
  Colonial style : creating classic interiors in your cape, colonial, or saltbox home / Treena Crochet.
    p. cm.
  ISBN 1-56158-622-6
  1. Interior decoration--United States. 2. Decoration and ornament, Early American.
  3. Architecture, Colonial--United States. 4. Dwellings--Remodeling--United States. I. Title.
  NK2003.C76 2005
  728'.37'0973028--dc22
                        2004011788

Printed in Singapore
10 9 8 7 6 5 4 3 2 1

The following manufacturers/names appearing in *Colonial Style* are trademarks: Jacuzzi®, Sub-Zero®

*To my sibs,
Barbara, Judy,
and David*

Acknowledgments

 WHOLEHEARTED THANKS to the many people at The Taunton Press, namely Helen Albert, executive editor, who brilliantly contributed to the text and sidebars, and photographer Randy O'Rourke, who patiently captured just the right shots, no matter how long they took. In addition, thanks to Editor Erica Sanders-Foege for her spirited editing that kept these pages alive. Thanks, also, to Wendi Mijal and Rosalind Wanke, whose creative talents produced a beautiful book, and to Jenny Peters for her coordination efforts.

A special thanks to all the homeowners who allowed Randy and me to take over their homes for the grueling two-day photo shoots and to the architects and interior designers who made it possible, especially my architect-friend, Peter LaBau, who listened emphatically as I formulated my ideas for writing this book.

Finally, I wish to acknowledge Virginia Commonwealth University School of the Arts in Qatar, which supported the writing of this book through a research grant.

Contents

Why Re-Create Classic Interiors?

Americans, like most, are romantics at heart. We love to look back on the past with the idea that life was simpler, somehow better. Proof of our nostalgia for the "good old days" is our appetite for houses from these times. It's no surprise that so many of our Colonial-, Cape Cod–, and Saltbox-style homes have been lovingly restored, renovated, or even built new—nor is it a surprise that so many of us want to take on such a project ourselves.

Unfortunately, the layout and amenities of Colonial-, Cape Cod–, or Saltbox-style homes are often outdated for the American family in the 21st century. Many, for example, have just one bathroom, which is hardly enough for most families these days. And, as our lifestyles have evolved, so has our use of space. Also, today we're comfortable with an eat-in-kitchen, preferably combined with a family room. In a classic Colonial home, this layout doesn't exist.

On the mental side of the equation, many homeowners are daunted by the idea of taking on such a monumental project. As an interior designer, I get asked all the time, "How can I restore my house to its pristine roots without giving up modern conveniences?" The answer is not an easy one. Whole books, magazines, and cable network shows are dedicated to the topic.

But as I tell my clients, no matter what the situation, there is always a solution. The most important step is uncovering the home's original bones. Then begins the planning process, where it's important to take into consideration the scope of work, budgetary constraints, time commitment, and finding the right specialists to carry out the work.

Undertaking any renovation job while remaining sensitive to the home's historic character can be stressful, costly, and disastrous if not carefully researched and planned. If you are thinking about renovating your period-style home, or even building a new one, this book will be a tremendous aid for you.

This book is meant to be used as a guide. Here, you'll find the ideas and tools to make smart decisions about undertaking such a

project with sensitivity to your home's historic character. In the following chapters, you'll find plenty of inspiring restorations and renovations that run the gamut from the near-museum-quality authentic to the more mainstream, to the very grand.

I'll begin by identifying and illustrating the major architectural hallmarks of the Colonial, Cape Cod, and Saltbox styles. Next, I'll discuss exterior and interior features most characteristic of the period, from rooflines and window placement to decorative details. Chapter 2 offers an in-depth look at woodwork typical of the Colonial period. In chapter 3, I'll cover more interior details, focusing on wall treatments and color schemes and also how to design ceilings and floors.

The final chapters examine updating the home for modern living. "Kitchens, Bathrooms, Storage, and Mudrooms" (chapter 4) looks at how to creatively expand or redesign your Colonial-style home, for example, by reconfiguring a bathroom or adding a modern kitchen. The last chapter examines how to create a classic interior, integrating modern amenities such as heating and cooling systems and lighting. Throughout the book, you'll find inspiring case studies that offer real-life solutions to updating and renovating questions.

Undertaking any renovation job while remaining sensitive to the home's historic character can be stressful, costly, and disastrous if not carefully researched and planned. It's my hope that this book will enlighten you about how to enjoy your vintage or vintage-style home while living a 21st-century lifestyle.

ONE

What Style Is Your Home?

COLONIAL ARCHITECTURE has set the standard for traditional housing in America for centuries. Old and new versions of this quintessentially New England–style home, with its distinctive box-shape plan and gabled roofline, can be found in communities far removed from the original colonies. The style's enduring popularity is more than nostalgia for the past.

Colonials, Cape Cods, and Saltboxes continue to appeal for both aesthetic and practical reasons. The Colonial façade has a pleasing symmetry reflecting the classical tastes of the 18th century. The floor plan of Colonial-style homes is eminently functional, even in today's world. And there is honesty in Colonial design born of pure practicality.

The early colonists needed to build efficiently for their own survival. Of necessity, they used locally available materials. An abundance of timber in the north provided the perfect material for frame construction and clapboard siding, while southern colonies utilized clay-rich soil to produce bricks. All the while running through the style of these early 17th-century houses is an essential quaintness, purity, and efficiency of design.

A testament to the Colonial style is its versatility. The basic architecture was adapted to the particular lifestyles and various climates. Regional differences determined the necessary preparations for either cold winters or hot, humid summers. In New England, a steeply pitched roofline allowed snow to slide off easily, and heavy

◀ Clapboards on the first Colonials were typically painted deep red, yellow ochre, or brown, or left unpainted. This white color is a 20th-century innovation that highlights the center hall's other classic features: symmetrically-arranged shuttered windows and chimneys, a gabled roof, and sidelights framing the front door. ▶ A transition away from the first-period Colonial style, this Georgian home has a front door that is flanked by classical pilasters and, like the sash windows, capped with a pediment.

Early Cape houses were built in stages as families grew. Building an addition for a half Cape like this one usually meant mirroring the existing structure to create a full Cape.

Typical woodwork details in traditional Colonial interiors feature wood floors, wainscoting, and crown molding along with door and window trim.

batten doors kept out harsh winds. Houses had small rooms with low ceilings, making them easier to heat. Small windows closed off with wooden shutters eliminated drafts. In warmer southern climates, larger windows were arranged to maximize cross ventilation, taking advantage of the breezes to counter the hot, humid summer temperatures. Louvered shutters kept the intense heat of the sun out, while letting in filtered light.

Apart from regional nuances, each architectural form within the style has distinctive features both inside and out that identify these homes as Colonials, Capes, or Saltboxes. Learning to recognize these hallmarks will help you better understand your own home's unique characteristics and choose the right details to enhance its charm.

EVOLUTION OF THE STYLE

The earliest Colonial houses began with one multipurpose room on the first floor and a sleeping or storage loft above. A fireplace located at one end of the room provided a hearth for cooking and became the sole source of heat during winter. As the homeowners needed more space, they expanded out from the basic box. To this day, the simple floor plan is a defining characteristic of Colonials.

By the 1700s, an evolving Cape Cod and Saltbox style emerged throughout New England as a variation on the basic Colonial theme. Capes were small in size, typically a one-and-a-half-story dwelling with a side gabled roof and centrally located front door and chimney. Saltboxes, identified by their distinctive sloping rooflines, developed from the expansion of the Colonial or Cape house by means of a one-story rear addition, called a lean-to. A roof over the new addition met the top of the ridgepole of the existing roof to give the rear of the house a steeper and more expansive profile.

With all three of these earlier styles, Colonial, Cape Cod, and Saltbox, decorative architectural details were minimal. As Americans achieved economic prosperity, their homes took on more decorative detailing, following contemporary trends in England. Georgian-style homes of the mid to late 18th century were well proportioned with formal classical elements positioned over entries and windows. The later Federal style developing at the end of the century reflected refined proportions and close articulation of the façade. In an attempt to modernize the Colonial aesthetic and to blend the original style with the emerging one, trimwork was added around windows and doors.

▼ **This Saltbox was built in 1998 by interior designer Nancy Kalin, who styled the house to appear completely authentic while furnishing it with carefully hidden state-of-the-art amenities.**

The Colonial Style

The front façade easily identifies these classic Colonial homes. These houses have two stories, a gabled roof, and central stairway. Although there are many variations on this theme, from a front gable to a side gable, most consistent is the placement of a central doorway that leads to a center hall and staircase. Rooms are organized off this center hall, usually two in the front and two in the back. Sash windows, symmetrically arranged and vertically aligned, appear on the first and second floors, and an additional window on the second-story landing balances the rhythm of the front door beneath it.

In the early days of colonial settlement, when nails were made by hand and every house was hand-built, Colonials were expanded as the budget and need for more space arose. Since these homes were not built all at once, the façade often lacked cohesiveness. The classical symmetry we have come to associate with Colonials is not always

▲ A modest mudroom connects the original 18th-century Colonial house to a barn, which now serves as the family media room.

▲ A two-story 18th-century Colonial in New Hampshire features a central chimney and side-gabled roof.

present in the earliest examples. Over time, rooms were added to one end or both of the first floors, or new additions were built behind the main house, often connecting it to the barn.

The style that inspires today's ideal "center-hall Colonial" emerged in the 18th century as a natural progression from a basic two-room house with center chimney to a four-room house, followed by a second story mirroring the configuration of the first floor. The Georgian house had two full stories, the second story replacing what had once been attic bedrooms. Heating the larger structure often required additional fireplaces and a second chimney. The entryway and stairway in this style of center-hall house was open and made a more impressive statement to visitors. To enhance the effect, the front entry was often decorated with pilasters and a pediment.

▲ **An elaborately detailed mantel, with its generous size, design, and carvings, reflects the wealth of the homeowner.**

Hallmarks of the Colonial Style

Early Colonial houses are modest in scale and use local materials such as clapboard, fieldstone, or brick in its construction, depending on region. Second-story sash windows are placed tightly under the eaves of a steeply gabled roof and may or may not have included shutters. Although early homes featured a central chimney, it was common to see two chimney stacks pushed to both sides on larger homes.

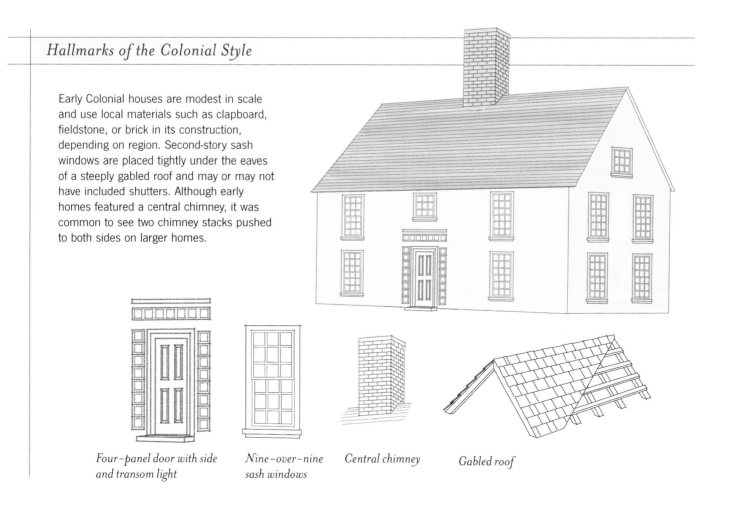

Four-panel door with side and transom light

Nine-over-nine sash windows

Central chimney

Gabled roof

The Cape Cod Style

The Cape Cod–style home is a more modest form of a Colonial than the Georgian house, which inspired today's center-hall Colonials. Capes began as simple two-room homes. As the loft was converted to bedrooms or sleeping rooms, dormer windows protruded from the steep pitch of the gabled roof, providing light and ventilation to the second level. A Cape was basically a one-and-a-half-story dwelling with a side gabled roof and, in a full Cape, a centrally located front door and chimney. Balancing off the main door was either one or a pair of casement or sash windows. The front-facing steep slope of the gabled roof might or might not have dormers.

The term "Cape Cod," as applied to this style home, originated in the 19th century to describe the compact clapboard houses of southern New England. In the mid-20th century, the Cape Cod style was a popular choice among suburban developers whose planned communities sprang up across America in the wake of World War II, supplying homes to young families of veterans.

▲ A stone wall remains as a reminder of the past in this renovated Cape and provides a texture that contrasts nicely with the formal painted woodwork.

◀ The Cape Cod style, a term first used in the 19th century to describe the clapboard houses of southern New England, with its one-and-a-half-story design, steeply gabled roof, and small and compact scale, is a clear descendant of the Colonial.

◀ Granite steps lead to a side door with an overhead transom that brings light into the inside hallway of this renovated Cape in New Hampshire.

Hallmarks of the Cape Cod Style

Capes are small, one- to one-and-a-half-story houses with two rooms on the lower level and sleeping rooms located in the attic space above. A central chimney projecting from the steeply gabled roof is linked to fireplaces in each of one-room-deep lower-level spaces. Early examples feature a batten-and-board front door with a glazed overhead transom. The house's compact design allows for expansion by duplicating the one-room-deep modular units on one or both sides.

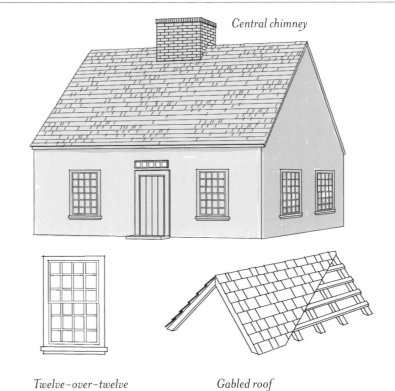

Central chimney

Batten-and-board door
with transom light

Twelve-over-twelve
sash windows

Gabled roof

The Saltbox Style

Saltboxes were named for the shape of the containers in which salt was sold in Colonial times. Although Saltboxes are usually associated with New England, historical examples are found in the South, where they are known as "Cat's Slide" houses. Both names refer to the distinctive roof shape of these homes.

Like Capes, these houses were the result of building on as need and economics dictated. These houses often started out as one-and-a-half-story Capes with shed bump-outs, or lean-tos, at the rear for kitchens. Many Saltboxes resulted when a first-floor addition was built onto a two-story house. Joining the roofline of the original structure with the new addition at the ridgepole left a roof longer and steeper at the back than in the front.

Hallmarks of the Saltbox Style

The quintessential Saltbox-style house developed from the expansion of smaller Colonials or Capes. As the need for more space arose, a small room built off of the back was connected to the main house with a lean-to roof. This unique design resembled containers used for salt at the time, hence the name.

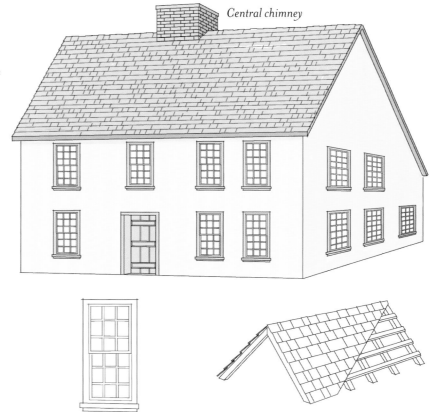

Central chimney

Batten-and-board door

Nine-over-nine sash windows

Asymmetrical gabled roof

◄ **The Saltbox form is clearly seen in this side view of the Prentis House on the property of the Shelburne Museum in Vermont.**

Saltboxes became so popular that by the end of the 17th century, new houses were built in the style. These homes, like Capes, were unassuming, especially compared to large Colonials. The exterior detailing usually followed suit. Entryways were often plain, though some grand examples can be found in New England.

▲ Characteristic of Saltbox-style houses, this 20th-century example captures the authenticity of the original style with its careful attention to detail: eight-over-twelve sash windows tucked tightly under the eaves, a central chimney, and a rear shed or cat's-slide roof.

Architectural Hallmarks

The gabled roof is most prominent on old Colonials with steep, sloping sides that limit the attic spaces within. In the Northeast, particularly areas around New York and Pennsylvania, the English tradition merged with a prevalent German ("Deutsch" was misunderstood to be "Dutch") influence, leading to the gambrel-style gable roof. Its shape is easily recognizable as it is often used on barns. The gambrel design raises the amount of space between floor and ceiling on the interior, giving more space for full-height walls.

▼ As is often the case, an old Colonial is expanded in a less-than-symmetrical manner. This main house connects to the barn via a two-story addition.

▶ Dormer windows projecting from the gabled roof bring light and ventilation to the attic space in this small Cape-style house, while finely detailed dentil molding runs just under the eaves.

While the exteriors of 17th-century homes were not painted, 18th-century examples had their clapboards painted in earth tones made from natural colorants or pigments such as iron oxide, raw sienna, burnt umber, or yellow ochre. Mixing colorants with milk made a durable paint for clapboards, window sashes, and doors to protect the wood.

From the one-room Colonial to the expansive Colonial Revival, the main door was usually accentuated by some architectural means. Early dwellings of the Pilgrims used a heavy batten-and-board door with overscaled wrought-iron hinges and hardware to keep the elements and animals at bay. By the early 18th century, the front entry incorporated small glazed transom panels above the front door and glass sidelights flanking its sides. Lintels, either flat or scrolled, began appearing over the front door in homes designed later in the 18th century.

▲ A newly built half Cape fits in perfectly with its surroundings on Cape Cod, Massachusetts.

▶ Bedrooms in early Colonial houses began as sleeping lofts in the attic spaces of the steeply pitched gabled roofs. Here, the original exposed rafters and ceiling boards add to the home's rustic charm.

▲ The asymmetrical front of this Colonial reflects the sequencing of its construction; the original house includes the front door and chimney, while rooms to the right were added as the need for additional space arose.

Dutch Colonial, Federal, and Revival Styles

The majority of early colonists came from England and brought their preference for English architecture and interiors with them. But the Germans (who in calling themselves "Deutsch"—the word for "German"—were mistaken for Dutch) also settled parts of the country, especially areas of New York and Pennsylvania. The gambrel roof, which came to be associated with the style, was not exclusively used in Dutch Colonials.

Federal-style houses emphasized a refinement of classical proportions and detailing. Popular after the American Revolution, Federal homes reflected the increasing wealth and prosperity of the owners. These houses were built on a larger scale to be more impressive. Windows were embellished with lintels and pediments. Most characteristic of the Federal style was the low-hipped roof and elaborate Palladian or fan windows above the front door and on the second- or third-story landing.

Colonial Revival style became popular as America celebrated its first centennial. A blend of the Colonial style with characteristics from later Georgian and Federal styles, Colonial Revival homes had a front portico supported by classical columns. The early 20th-century houses featured a first floor with rooms (including a kitchen) located off a central hallway and stairwell, while the bedrooms and a bathroom were located in a full second story.

▲ Colonial Revival–style homes remained popular from the centennial of 1876, when they were first introduced, through the 1930s. Ionic columns on the front porch reflect the influence of the short-lived Greek Revival styles of the 1820s and 1830s.

An entry door and pediment with a fan light is characteristic of the Federal style.

Built in 1830 as a new addition to an existing 1708 Colonial, a prominent gambrel roof sets it apart from other period homes in its North Andover, Massachusetts, neighborhood.

A low-hipped roof with two chimneys frames the symmetrical façade in this newly built Federal home. The understated elegance of the exterior is common with those homes built in the rural areas surrounding Boston and Salem, where local architects Charles Bulfinch and Samuel McIntire made the style popular.

Slender columns form the portico of a Colonial Revival home.

Interior Details

▲ Original ceiling beams were left exposed when this house was restored. A four-panel door features authentic iron thumb-latch hardware.

Colonial homes built prior to 1750 had humble beginnings with their low ceilings, plaster walls, exposed timber beams, wide-plank floors, and sparse furnishings. Eventually, wood paneling left in a natural finish covered walls surrounding the fireplace to make it easier to wipe off the soot. The simplicity of these early homes is favored by many seeking to replicate the rustic flavor of the early Colonial era.

After 1750, larger houses that featured more architectural detail reflected the prosperity of their owners. Wood-paneled walls, interior trimwork, including moldings and boxed beams, turned balusters for staircases, and carved fireplace mantels were painted, giving the interiors a more refined appearance. Although rooms were more spacious and had higher ceilings, proportion and scale was carefully weighed against the amount of detailing included in them.

Low interior ceilings and the steep pitch of the gabled roof required windows to be placed tightly under the eaves on the second story. Most of the earliest Colonials lacked glazing since leaded glass had to be imported from England and the cost was prohibitive. Instead, wooden shutters kept out the rain and cold weather. As settlements developed and the colonists prospered, glass casement windows that swung open and closed like shutters were used. Later, the sash window became popular.

▶ The entry hall in this 1680s Colonial shows just how steep the staircases were as steps eventually replaced ladders to reach the sleeping lofts above.

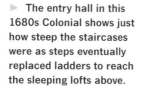

A Rustic Colonial

Prior to 1750, timbers used to support the second floor were left exposed, while wood paneling placed around the fireplace was painted to make it easier to wipe off layers of soot.

Vertical floor-to-ceiling wood paneling

Exposed, rough-hewn beams

Low ceiling

Shaped moldings forming the mantelpiece

Dutch oven

Wide-plank flooring

Christian cross door with iron latch

A Classic Colonial

The late Colonial style is more refined with its painted gun-stock corner posts, boxed beamed ceilings, raised paneling, and wide pine flooring.

Painted boxed beams

Gunstock corner post

Crown molding

Reflective light fixture

Raised paneling

Wide pine flooring

Plaster wall
treatment

▲ Classic dentil
molding and a
featured rosette
captures Georgian
styling.

WOODWORK

With all three styles, Colonial, Cape Cod, and Saltbox, decorative architectural details were minimal. As Americans achieved economic prosperity, houses took on more decorative detailing following contemporary trends in England. Georgian-styled homes of the mid to late 18th century were well proportioned with formal classical elements positioned over entries and windows. The later Federal style developing at the end of the century reflected refined proportions and fine articulation of the façade. In an attempt to modernize the Colonial houses, trimwork around windows and doors was later added as a means to blend the old style with the new.

◄ Imported blue
tiles adorn the
surround of this
Georgian-style
mantel.

A Grand Georgian

Classical detailing enhances the beauty of
this living room, showing off the elegance
of the Georgian interior.

Painted
boxed beams

Corner cabinet built-in with
dentil molding and pilasters

Classical
clamshell design

Raised paneling

Blue-and-white imported tile surround

◀ The fireplace in this upstairs bedroom is simple in design and detailing compared with the fire-places found in the more formal downstairs living and dining rooms.

▼ Narrow, pine strip floor-ing is more common in Colonial homes of the late 19th century.

WALLS, CEILINGS, AND FLOORS

Gradually, the interior use of color became a cultural artifact. By the 18th century, color was prominently used on the woodwork around beams, on fireplace mantels, and on wainscoting to enhance the decorative details. Later, Federal-style Colonials included painted plaster walls and trim.

As early as 1810, some walls featured scenic wallpapers. The later Colonial Revival styles of the late 19th and early 20th centuries celebrated wallpaper in every room.

Softwood and hardwood such as heart pine or chestnut dominated as the primary flooring material in all Colonial homes and was often

▲ A view from the original front parlor reveals two subsequent additions to this Federal home first built in 1810.

▲ An early keeping room features a cooking hearth and beehive oven.

protected with handmade oil cloths in early times. Fine oriental carpets were used in more prosperous times.

The refinement of Colonial homes continued in the treatment of the ceiling; by the Federal period, boxed beams were hidden. Fine plaster ceiling medallions adorned dining rooms and parlors.

KITCHENS, BATHS, MUDROOMS, AND STORAGE

From the humble one-room dwellings to the multiple rooms of the early Colonials, the cooking hearth became a prominent feature of the home. In early examples of smaller homes, a centrally located fireplace was enough to provide heat for the home and possessed a large enough hearth for cooking. As the Georgian style developed and larger homes were built, two chimneys, pushed to the end walls, each with a downstairs and upstairs fireplace, doubled the heating capacity. Kitchens were pushed to outbuildings or "keeping rooms" in the rear.

Since indoor plumbing is a relatively recent addition to American homes, bathrooms were nonexistent in Colonial times, but they were a feature in the Colonial Revival. For plumbing fixtures in kitchens and baths, homeowners should look to the Colonial Revival as a source of inspiration. Cabinetry details can be derived from the interior woodwork in other parts of the house.

Storage was handled quite differently in early America for the simple reason that people didn't have the volume of stuff to store. Historic homes often have charming built-ins but dismally little, if any, closet space. To make useable closets, many homeowners claim space under the eaves or turn an undersized bedroom into a walk-in closet.

▲ The living room in this Colonial built in 1708 has been modified to accommodate a media cabinet and surround-sound speakers.

▲ A row of sash windows brings in natural light and the outdoors in this newly built Colonial kitchen.

▲ An expansive living room captures Colonial charm with its twelve-over-twelve sash windows, wide pine flooring, and up-to-code fireplace.

Colonial Cooling

Owning a Colonial home doesn't mean living in Colonial times. In fact, most homeowners take advantage of air-conditioning systems that are available today. HVAC systems, another option, rely on small, flexible tubing to distribute warmth or coolness to rooms from air handlers placed in the cellar and attic. Although they are costlier than other types of central air-conditioning or forced-air heating, homeowners choose them because they are less noticeable and can be installed without major reconfiguring.

A cast-iron radiator provides heat throughout a long New England winter. Air-conditioning for summertime cooling is distributed through the small, round floor vent.

TODAY'S CLASSIC INTERIOR

Indoor plumbing was nonexistent in the American Colonial era—imagine what people of that time would have thought about big-screen plasma TVs, microwaves, and air-conditioning? Integrating these conveniences of the 21st century with a style that originated more than three centuries ago is one of the biggest challenges for the owner of a period style home.

The good news is that you don't have to sacrifice the modern amenities we take for granted in order to have a traditional look in your home. The great interest in historically sensitive renovation has created a boom of suppliers who offer clever ways to disguise heating and air-conditioning sources or the components of a home-theater system. You can enclose a circuit-breaker panel behind a wooden door that blends perfectly with surrounding Colonial-style detailing. Hiding other signs of modern life is always necessary, though. Matching color schemes on appliances with period-appropriate interiors, for example, works well. Blending is often as good a solution and will offer you more options in choosing services and appliances.

▲ An old sewing machine cabinet makes for a creative solution for a sink vanity in this cozy half bath.

◄ The homeowners of this small Cape still prefer to dine by candlelight, evidenced by the reproduction chandelier hanging from the ceiling beam.

TWO

Woodwork

COLONIAL, CAPE COD, OR SALTBOX house may be easy to spot from the outside, but it's not uncommon to discover that its interior is completely out of keeping with the period and style. In old houses that have survived remodels or renovations, it's often the woodwork that's the first to go. But repairs to the doors, windows, mantels, moldings, stairs, and cabinetry often result in a home's architectural character becoming obscured or even erased altogether as the interior takes on a style far different from the period.

Returning a Colonial, Cape Cod, or Saltbox home to its original beauty often means looking to the architectural designs that prevailed during Colonial times. Although the style was popular from the 1600s to the late 1700s (and revived in the early 1900s), the architectural trends remained fairly consistent. American builders during this time produced work closely following styles from their English heritage, with modifications made based on available labor and resources.

Early woodwork designs featured simple profiles for crown moldings, on door and window trim, and on fireplace mantels. As the 18th century progressed, the prosperity of the colonists increased. Later Georgian and American Federal woodwork became more intricate (and required a higher degree of craftsmanship). This elaborate decoration, reserved for "public" rooms where guests were welcomed, was meant to convey the wealth and social status of the owner.

◀ This sitting room illustrates classic 18th-century Colonial woodwork. Boxed ceiling beams and a salvaged six-panel door create a more refined look, while wainscoting adds a protective finish to the plaster walls. ▶ This wall paneling is a perfect example of hand-planed millwork characteristic of rustic Colonials.

For example, within the Colonial, Cape Cod, and Saltbox styles, highly profiled and carved crown moldings, shaped chair rails, and decorative mantels were saved for the sitting room in the front of the house. In private rooms such as the keeping room (or kitchen) and bedrooms, money was not wasted on decorative woodwork.

So, even though one often looks for clues about replaced or missing woodwork profiles throughout an old house, when restoring a Colonial, Cape, or Saltbox, it's important to keep in mind how the space in the house was divided—public and private.

The moldings in the back of the house, where servants worked and lived, for example, were simpler than those in the front parlor or sitting room. But within public and private living spaces, the woodwork is unified. Doors match windows, moldings match mantels, and stairs match trimwork to build a cohesive design within each particular area of the home. Stylistic detail and materials used in harmony set the theme for how these elements are echoed from room to room.

Stylistic signatures on other woodwork, such as crown moldings and baseboards, related to how doors were framed as well. The lintel over a doorway was often fashioned after the crown-molding profile, although it may have been scaled down to fit the size of the door or cased opening. Crown-molding designs also impacted the shape and proportion of a fireplace mantel. Window seats, wall paneling, corner cabinets,

◀ In this 18th-century Cape, wall paneling complements the six-panel door, while crown molding defines the ceiling. The slender newel post and baluster design balance a shaped handrail.

A Georgian Touch

WHEN THE HOMEOWNERS of a New England Cape decided to expand their living space to accommodate a large combination breakfast–reading room, they decided to focus on the home's later Georgian influences. Built-out bookcases incorporate crown moldings with dentils carved into the frieze area. The molding continues uninterrupted across the length of the wall, creating a cornice for the windows. Casement windows running from floor to ceiling crank open to capture and direct breezes, while the divided-light panels maintain a sense of Colonial style.

A new addition features a series of floor-to-ceiling casement windows, which open the interior to grand hilltop views.

and cupboards often incorporated the same profiles, making them appear to be a seamless part of the architecture.

When planning a renovation or restoration of a Colonial, Cape, or Saltbox, examine the architectural detailing still in place in areas such as exterior doors and windows, stairs, and built-ins for clues. This helps in reading how authentic the remaining woodwork details are in the rest of the house.

Taking any one of these elements out of context disrupts the flow of the space and destroys the unity of the home's design. It's here where one finds the source of design inspiration for these beautiful homes. And it's here where one can begin to know what's appropriate and inappropriate in restoring or remodeling them.

Although today a Colonial style may no longer have strictly public and private space, it's important to keep in mind that woodwork detail in some rooms of the house should reflect a certain formality and in other rooms should be used to create a more rustic or simple look.

▲ **Molding creates the mantel with a simple cornice and smooth frieze. The side pilaster is decorated with recessed panel shaft and basic capital design, also seen in the cornice.**

Windows

As glass was a scarcity, the first windows in Colonial homes were simply unglazed openings protected by wooden shutters. (And when available, parchment, a translucent paper, was used.) These movable window covers not only kept out the elements but also protected the home's inhabitants from animals and intruders.

When glass became more widely available and less expensive, the shutter design evolved into the casement window. Hinged on the sides, these windows swung open like shutters and were fitted with small panes of diamond-shaped glass held in place with lead muntins, which was a common element seen in English cottages.

By the 1700s, sash windows with sliding upper and lower panels were more popular in Colonial houses. Each sash was divided into twelve panes of glass held in place with wooden muntins, and as glassmakers mastered larger pieces of glass, the number of panes was reduced to nine, six, and eventually four. But muntins remained integral to the design.

The woodwork around windows followed the general trim profiles used within the rest of the house. Window casings typically echoed door trim, often shaped with a small bead. Usually, an appropriately scaled top casing emulated the same cornice detail found on the lintels above door openings.

Hardware used on the casings was a simple sash lock made from wrought iron or, in finer houses, brass.

Although homeowners of Colonial-, Cape-, and Saltbox-style houses are tempted to replace these sash locks with decorative examples from the Victorian period, it's inappropriate to replace them with anything fancier.

▲ Shutters without glass windows were used in Colonial homes until the late 19th century.

▲ Sash windows with sliding lower panels are a strong characteristic of Colonial-style homes.

Windows: Out with the Old?

It's been said that replacing windows saves energy and cuts down on maintenance. But don't assume you have to replace the windows just because you own a period home. Recent research shows that traditional double-hung windows, in conjunction with storm windows, work just as well as today's insulated ones. Of course, this is an expense you can't avoid if the windows function poorly or have been weather damaged.

Snap-In Muntins

With the exception of Dutch Colonial style, which sometimes featured casement windows, the double-hung window with multiple small panes held by muntins is synonymous with Colonial style. In some parts of the house, especially in sunrooms, casement windows provide superior ventilation and ease of opening and closing, particularly in humid weather. Because Colonial architecture remains popular in new construction, window manufacturers offer a full range of Colonial-style windows, including casement and awning types. The moldings around the thermal glass are Colonial in inspiration, and optional snap-in muntins complete the divided-light look.

▼ Colonial Revival homes take advantage of improved glassmaking techniques, featuring larger glass panes.

◄ Casement windows swing open to give an unobstructed view to the outdoors.

In Keeping with a Cape

WHEN THE OWNERS OF AN 18TH-CENTURY
Cape decided to expand the house by building a new addition, they took the opportunity to make some necessary changes to the original keeping room (or kitchen) at the same time. Adding a bay window to one wall expanded the small size of the keeping room, providing light and ventilation to an otherwise closed-in space.

A new bay window with divided-light panels brings new life to an otherwise small and dark space.

► **Hung over each window's lower section, louvered shutters provide privacy in this bedroom while keeping the upper sash open to view the outdoors.**

The symmetry of Colonials, such as this 1810 home with nine-over-six window sashes, is maintained by pairing windows within each room.

Perfect Storm Windows

There is an aesthetically pleasing way to add storm windows to historic homes without having to resort to the aluminum, prefabricated kind. This resourceful homeowner first designed a special frame to fit the outside dimensions of the window. Next, the frame was divided into an upper and a lower sash, matching the alignment of the sash of the interior window. The frame was then attached to the top of the window with hinges, leaving the bottom open for an easy escape in case of fire. A wrought-iron handle was added to the frame, making it convenient to transport it to the cellar for storage.

This removable storm window provides excellent thermal control as air trapped between it and the interior window insulates against the cold.

Shutter Style

IN COLONIAL TIMES, the most practical way of keeping weather, animals, and intruders at bay was through wooden shutters. A variety of
shutter forms appeared throughout Colonial architecture including solid-
panel, raised-panel, and louvered designs. Indian shutters, regional
nomenclature identifying a type of shutter that slides into the wall cavity
when not in use, were popular throughout the Colonial period. Folding
shutters in either solid- or raised-panel designs were placed on the inside,
offering complete control for opening and closing. Exterior shutters of this
design were purely decorative and are synonymous with Colonial styling.
In the South, louvered shutters were more popular because they could be
adjusted to filter in light while shielding the hot sun. Their louvered
designs also allowed for light breezes to pass through from the outside.

▲ **Original Indian
shutters in this
1708 home are
still used by the
homeowners today
to keep out winter
drafts. The ingen-
iously designed
shutter slides
from inside the
wall and creates a
strong hold against
forced entry.**

◄ **Accordion-fold
shutters add elegant
woodwork detail to
the windows.**

IN HISTORY

Hinged on its side, a casement window cranks open like a swinging door. Often grouped in pairs, casement windows enable the capture of breezes from the outside and provide directional airflow and ventilation to the interior. Casement windows were often seen in the earliest Colonial houses before the invention of the sash window.

◀ A prominent cornice projects from this overhead lintel, while wide trim frames the sides of the window in this restored Cape in New Hampshire.

▼ In southern climates, windows were designed to take advantage of cooling breezes and are scaled much larger than those in the Northeast. These Colonial-period windows run nearly floor to ceiling and feature three movable sashes.

Doors

From the most basic designs to the elaborate, the front door of a Colonial home sets the tone for what's to be found inside. Their architectural roots in the one-room house, these doors at first were simple. They grew in their mass and level of detail as the style evolved and colonists prospered.

One of the earliest types of doors was the board-and-batten style. Wide boards of wood were cut to fit the door's opening and held in place by narrow strips of wood called batten. These were used inside the home as well, as the overall interior was also more rustic in its style and design. A glazed transom was typically placed overhead, bringing light into the front entry.

▲ The trim around this six-panel door follows the profile of the crown molding, while a small wainscot cap balances the weight of the baseboard in this Massachusetts Colonial.

◄ An original batten door remains in the upstairs bedroom, which dates to 1708. Simply constructed from planks of wood, batten doors were the most basic door type of early Colonials.

◄ A pair of raised-panel doors was copied from drawings of earlier Colonial styles in this new home. Reproduction hardware, easily available today, captures authentic styling.

IN HISTORY

A simple architectural element, the muntin was the prevalent structural support for window glass. Muntins were made from a variety of materials, including stone and lead—as seen in Medieval church windows—and later, wood.

Before sheet glass, glazing was made from flattened balloons of molten glass, giving each pane a circular shape or "bull's-eye" design. The pliable nature of lead made it easy to follow these small, round shapes of the blown glass. Proven to work in stained glass, lead muntins were quickly adapted for use in windows for houses.

In the 18th century, glassmaking techniques advanced, resulting in the production of rolled glass. The glazing was made into long cylinders, then cut lengthwise and rolled flat into sheets. Wood muntins were used to hold these square panes in place, creating small, gridlike patterns.

Later homes designed in the 18th century often featured a solid-wood front door with a raised-panel design in either a four- or six-panel configuration. Along with an overhead transom, homes designed in the second half of the 18th century often incorporated sidelights flanking the front door, which also gave direct view to the outside. Because large pieces of glass were a rare commodity, glazing in the transom and sidelights was compartmentalized into small, squared panes held in place with wood muntins.

▲ Sidelights and an overhead transom frame this six-panel front door, allowing a clear view to the outside in this original Newburyport, Massachusetts, Colonial.

▲ Often called a "Christian cross" door, this four-paneled door gets its name from the pattern made by its inner supporting members.

HARDWARE

Hardware was chosen for its practicality, its availability, and, when possible, to complement the door's design features. At the time, metal for hardware was difficult to come by, so it was often recycled from barrel staves or farm implements. Colonial styles made use of wrought-iron thumb latches, typically the design creation of the local blacksmith.

This indigenous talent resulted in the production of a variety of styles. The most common, called the bean Suffolk, got its name from the beanlike shape at the top of the handle. Other common designs incorporated a spear or heart shape.

Latches were used on both outside and inside doors until doorknobs were invented and widely available—most often imported from England or fashioned by hand locally. While thumb latches were common in the more rustic Colonials, doorknobs made from iron, brass, or porcelain were indicative of finer homes.

Replacement Doors

Colonial, Cape, and Saltbox homes are often missing original doors. These days, finding new replacements is easier because, due to the popularity of the Colonial style, door manufacturers are reintroducing a variety of traditional styles. Otherwise, look for salvaged antique doors—more of a challenge, but worth it for their aged beauty and dense woods. Start your search in areas saturated with Colonials, Capes, or Saltbox houses.

▶ Layers of paint have been stripped from this three-panel door still fitted with its original hardware. The door connects a bedroom from the 1708 part of the house with an addition that dates to about 1830.

The outside batten door protects an inner door against the weather. A transom panel located above the door is a common feature of Colonial homes that brings light into the entry vestibule.

This house experienced so much settling over the years that the six-panel door, with its original thumb-latch hardware, had to be planed and rehung in order for it to open and close properly.

A Colonial blacksmith left his mark on the style of this bean Suffolk thumb latch in the form of an intricate star design forged onto the handle of this reproduction.

▲ Colonial Revival–style houses, which are more formal in their design, incorporate pocket doors to close off the dining area from the living room.

The Bean Suffolk Latch

Borrowing from English practicality, Colonial doors were secured with iron thumb latches fashioned into a variety of designs. Most popular amongst the American colonists was the bean Suffolk, the name combining both the shape of the handle plate with the region in England where it was commonly found. Variations abound as blacksmiths from various parts of England incorporated regional designs such as the spear, heart, tulip, or swordfish motifs into their hardware for doors and cabinetry.

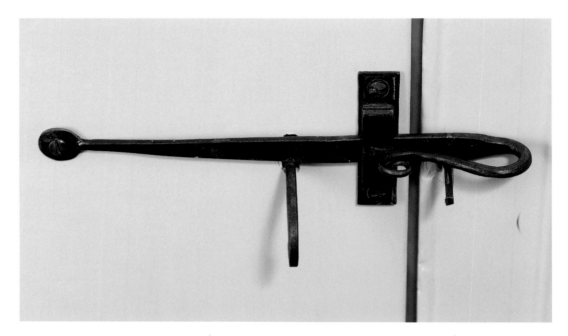

► When pressed, the thumb latch on the opposite side of this door raises the slender and elegantly curved bar, releasing it from its catch.

▲ Placement of the H-hinge required doors to be hung flush with their trim.

IN HISTORY

Strap hinges are the earliest form of Colonial door hinge. Since iron was scarce in the young colonies, strap hinges were often made from old wagon tires or reshaped oxshoes. The limited number of local smiths and the rapid growth of communities meant that large quantities of hardware had to be imported from England or the Continent. The butterfly, or dovetail, hinge is found from New England to Pennsylvania.

By far the most popular hinge style was the H-hinge and its variation, the H-L–hinge. Legend has it that the "H" stood for "holy," and that the H-hinges helped protect the house dwellers against witchcraft.

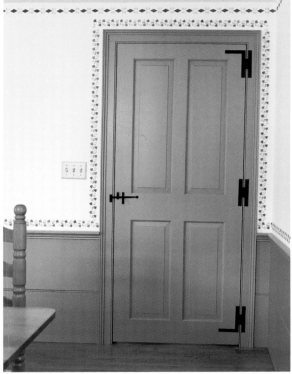

The door hardware utilizes basic H-hinges and a common latch lock.

◄ A transom panel above the back door of this Cape is fitted with bull's-eye glass panes. The swirling pattern, which gives the glass its name, is a result of the blown glass being flattened into a disk during the process.

▼ Variations of thumb-latch designs include the spade shape seen in this example. Other designs include the bean Suffolk, arrowhead Suffolk, and heart Suffolk.

▶ A white porcelain doorknob provides basic utility for this Christian cross door.

▲ This brass thumb latch reflects the wealth of the original homeowner: a ship captain from Portsmouth, New Hampshire.

◀ A rare thumb latch incorporates both iron and pewter in its unusual and highly decorative design.

IN HISTORY

Colonial blacksmiths contributed to the development of the American colonies by using a valuable natural resource, bog iron. Blacksmiths took the material from the marshes of New England and attempted without success to use it. Colonists were forced to buy iron imported from England for, among other things, their door and window hardware, horseshoes, and farm implements. In the meantime, colonists continued to develop the natural resources. By 1750, more highly skilled Colonial blacksmiths were producing iron. The development of ironworks aided in winning the American Revolution, as artillery could finally be made at home.

Architectural Trim

Architectural trim developed from the rough-hewn timbers that were used to support the earliest Colonial homes. As styles became less rustic and more refined, primitive beams and corner posts were translated into crown moldings and trimwork around doors and windows.

Trimwork in the Colonial style varies in its decoration depending on its location within the home. For example, in the public rooms such as the front entry, staircase, living room, and dining room, the milling of wood for crown moldings, baseboards, door and window trim, fireplace surrounds, and mantel was more decorative. The private rooms such as bedrooms and the upstairs hallway feature more simplistic details.

In Colonials, Capes, and Saltbox homes, the architectural trim was carefully scaled to fit the proportions of the room, taking into

▲ Architectural trimwork evolves from the rough-hewn beams and posts that were left exposed in early Colonial homes.

▼ In the earliest Colonial homes, the structural framework was left exposed then filled in with plaster for insulation.

consideration the ceiling heights and overall room dimensions. Smaller Colonials and Capes used simple molding styles and trims so rooms remained clean and uncluttered. Classically based Colonial styles like Georgian and Federal homes and later Colonial Revival styles had higher ceilings and, in order to be seen from the distance below, featured more ornate or complex moldings.

The partially exposed ceiling beam running along the perimeter of early Colonial homes was the origin for what we know today as decorative crown molding.

▲ Understated moldings and trimwork frame the openings of the fireplace and windows in this early Colonial home.

▲ This paneling shows how walls became more elaborate as the style evolved, with its picture-frame panels that create an even rhythm in this bedroom. The mantel duplicates the molding design and shows fine craftsmanship in its mitered corners.

▲ The furring out of rough-hewn timber beams became popular during the Georgian style of Colonial design, giving the home's interior a more refined look.

Gunstock Corner Posts

Gunstock posts take their name from the tapering shape of a rifle butt and are the most basic supporting member of frame construction so common with Colonial buildings. Over time, the rough posts were concealed behind a furred-out column, bringing symmetry and refinement to the home's interior. Gunstock corner posts disappeared from view completely with the introduction of the Federal style.

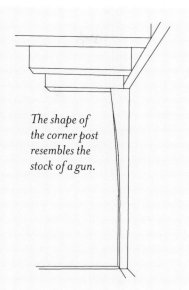

The shape of the corner post resembles the stock of a gun.

▼ A fully paneled wall surrounding the fireplace meets with the supporting gunstock corner post in this restored Colonial from the mid-18th century. The yellow ochre paint accentuates the room's woodwork and unifies the room.

From Trim to Molding

Moldings and trim add a touch of elegance to the Colonial interior, a refinement of style and taste over the rough-hewn timber beams and gun-stock corner posts that came before. Trim around windows and doors often followed the same profile as exterior trim, scaled according to the room's size and ceiling height for the interior. Whether flat with a small bead or a gently shaped ogee profile, trim and moldings are common in the later Georgian, Federal, and Colonial Revival styles.

▲ Exterior molding running along the eaves of this Colonial-style home translates into crown molding on the inside.

◄ Covering the exposed rough-hewn timber beams that ran along the perimeter of the Colonial home, crown molding like this was added to Colonial interiors to even out the rough transition between wall and ceiling.

▲ The arched opening between a newly remodeled kitchen and breakfast room features trimwork in the classically based designs of mid-18th-century Georgian-style homes. Removed from its original location in the front living room, the arch accentuates classical detailing seen on the flanking bookcase.

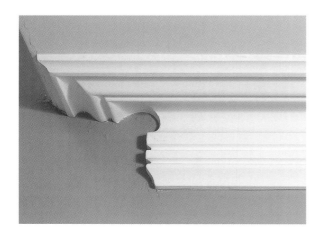

As ceiling heights increased in the Federal and Colonial Revival styles, crown moldings and architectural trimwork took on greater prominence, becoming more massive and more decorated.

Basic Molding Shapes

Today's standard "Colonial" window and door casing is just one example of what was once a wider range of molding options. Before the invention of power tools, moldings were cut with molding planes designed to cut an amazing variety of shapes. Combining several basic shapes could yield an entirely new profile. Today, routers and shapers take the place of molding planes and local custom mill shops, given a sample, can reproduce nearly any Colonial molding.

Ogee

Quirk Bead

Ovolo

Classic Elegance

After 1750, larger Colonial houses were built with more elaborate architectural details to reflect the prosperity of its owner. Interior trimwork, including moldings, chair rails, and carved fireplace mantels, incorporated classical design elements inspired by the more popular Georgian designs seen in England. Architectural trim was painted in lighter colors to give the interiors a more refined appearance and accentuated architectural details, which were carefully weighed against the amount of detailing included in a room.

◀ An intricate reed pattern appears in the chair rail of this Colonial home. The motif is carried throughout the room in the ceiling molding, as well as in smaller details on the mantel of the fireplace.

▼ This fireplace design shows elegant detailing with its classically proportioned pilaster, plinth and mantel.

Stairs

Stairways in Colonials, Cape Cod, and Saltbox houses were an important part of the home's design. More than a means of getting from the first floor to the second floor, stairs made a lasting impression upon those who entered the front door. Depending on the size of the home or when it was first built, stair designs varied from the small and steep to the wide and grand.

Early staircases fit tight into the entry hall. They were narrow and steep, turning one or two times before reaching the second story. These early designs utilized the most basic structural elements: a newel

▶ A staircase in the front entry hall of this Saltbox-style home features a squared-off newel post with a simple cap at each landing.

◀ ▲ Banister and balusters are balanced by a chamfered newel post. Simple, turned balusters shift the emphasis onto the newel post.

post and simple balusters to support the banister with unadorned stringers supporting the stairs. In the larger-scaled Federal and Colonial Revival styles, the entry hall featured a straight run of stairs, accentuated by elaborately carved woodwork on balusters, stringers, and newel posts.

Whether in a rustic or refined house, newel posts were generally emphasized as a prominent element, incorporating either squared-off posts with a plinth base and top cap or featuring elaborate turnings. In early Colonials, balusters were shaped into simple, rounded spindles, but as the later Georgian, Federal, and Colonial Revival styles became more classically influenced, their shapes grew markedly detailed.

◄ ▼ A crowning achievement in staircase design, this mid-19th-century example features a hefty newel post, elaborate stringer designs, and uniformly shaped balusters. The baseboards are larger to balance the visual weight and mass of the stairs.

Stair Repair

In the Colonial period, woodturning was its own trade producing everything from stair balusters to bedposts. Matching a damaged stair spindle or post can be challenging. But an Internet search of "custom turning" will yield many leads to woodturners who can match the profile. Once mechanized turning came into wide practice, stair parts became more standardized, so Colonial Revival–style turnings are easier to match through stock producers.

◄ The back staircase in this new Colonial home incorporates basic utility in its squared newel posts and plain balusters.

▲ Staircases in early Colonial homes took up little space as they evolved from a simple ladder used to access the sleeping loft. The space-saving technique of a U-shaped stair configuration with winders at each turn resulted in steep, compact stairs, making them more treacherous than later examples.

Code Check

If you find yourself having to replace a stairway due to unstable structural support, be sure to contact your local code-enforcement agency. Municipalities require that all new staircases meet specific safety codes, such as riser heights, tread depths, handrail height, and baluster spacing to protect against personal injury. Some cities and towns offer exemptions or variances for historic houses, determined by the officiating code officer.

▶ **The introduction of a straight run of stairs occurs in the larger designs of later Georgian, Federal, and Colonial Revival styles. Here, the entry hall is extended to the full length of the staircase.**

Cape with a Column

UNHAPPY WITH A CRAMPED FRONT ENTRY HALL,
the homeowners of this small Cape consulted an architect for
suggestions on what to do. They decided to open and connect the entry hall to the living area by replacing a load-bearing
wall with a structural column. Recessed paneling added to
the stairway creates a more interesting surface treatment and
adds a new focal point from the living room.

**An enclosed entry
hall is opened up
to the living room,
giving full view into
the staircase.**

Making an Entrance

TURNING WHAT WAS FIRST BUILT as a duplex in 1810 into a one-family residence challenged both architect and homeowner in how to treat the new front stairwell. After studying countless drawing books on period style, the homeowners selected a few details found in some of the finer Federal homes indigenous to New England. The result features a combination of elements that is both inspiring and classic in detailing and proportions.

▲ Stair stringers feature delicately shaped skirting details, which were based on sketches by the homeowner. Pendants with acorn nodes balance out the detail work.

◄ The homeowners opted for an elegant scroll supported by a cluster of balusters instead of a newel post to create a more sophisticated design.

▲ Before continuing up two steps to the large second-story hallway, the stairs take a pause at the top with a small landing. The banister's gentle sweep is echoed in the articulation of the wainscot wall.

Built-In Furniture

These older homes rarely had built-ins, and if they did, the storage was limited to a closet tucked neatly alongside the chimney flue, maybe a cupboard built into the corner of the front parlor for displaying the owner's collection of pewterware, and perhaps a window seat or two.

In a time when furniture was expensive and rare, built-ins were a practical way of providing storage space in the Colonial home. The designs of built-ins incorporated many of the same features as the architectural woodwork; crown moldings topped off corner cabinets, while glass fronts mimicked the muntin designs of windows. Even window seats incorporated the same articulation as the wainscoting with either recessed or raised panels.

Window seats were found in Colonial homes dating back to the mid-18th century. Their function served two purposes: one as a means of gaining additional storage space without additional furniture, and they provided a place to sit. A hinged lid made for easy access to the storage area below that blended design and detailing with the room's wainscoting.

▲ By the early 18th century, cupboards were built as recesses in the wall and often flanked the fireplace. Here, raised-panel doors open to reveal the family's china.

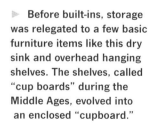

▶ Before built-ins, storage was relegated to a few basic furniture items like this dry sink and overhead hanging shelves. The shelves, called "cup boards" during the Middle Ages, evolved into an enclosed "cupboard."

▲ Cupboards in early Colonial homes featured open shelving placed tight against a wall for support. This example is fitted with drawers and a side compartment for additional storage.

Built-in cabinets had humble beginnings in the formal parlors of homes designed in the mid to late 18th century. Then, cabinets were used to display the family's collection of imported china, a prized possession. Today, we tend to rely on cabinets to hide modern conveniences ranging from computers to televisions and stereo equipment.

▲ Classical pilasters frame this cabinet set into the corner of the dining room. The arched glass front completes a classical theme more common with the late Colonial styles of the Georgian and Federal periods.

▶ The design for this new corner cabinet was taken from Colonial examples.

Restoring Built-Ins

 xtra care should be taken when restoring original built-ins such as cupboards and cabinets, especially when designs incorporate rolled-glass windows. Since these built-ins have sensitive hardware mechanisms, contact your local historical society to obtain a listing of qualified restorers in your area, specifically artisans who specialize in antique furniture repair. On the other hand, be careful when restoring woodwork not to ruin its aged patina.

▲ The room's architectural molding styles around windows and doors reflect the refinement of the late Colonial style also seen in the broken pediment top of the corner cabinet.

▶ Small shafts of space running alongside the chimney flue were designated closet spaces in early Colonial homes.

▼ A window seat still provides valuable space for storage and sitting while maintaining the charm of an antique Cape.

Adding Cabinets

When adding a built-in cabinet to a vintage-style home, gather ideas from the architectural elements found in other areas of the house. A batten door with H-hinges and a thumb latch might serve perfectly well on a built-in cabinet used in a bathroom for linen storage, but for those tricky retractable doors accommodating media equipment, a batten door may be too thick to slide into the slender side channels. A door of mortise-and-tenon construction would be more accommodating and can be designed to blend in by using hardware styles similar to others in the home.

The owners decided to use a door salvaged from their original 1760s Cape for the cupboard in their new breakfast room.

To get more storage space, the homeowners used the narrow space alongside the original 1708 cooking hearth to locate a new closet.

A small closet features a simple board-and-batten door held shut by a wooden latch.

THREE

Walls, Ceilings, and Floors

HE COLONIAL-STYLE INTERIOR is such a part of American culture that it's virtually synonymous with "old house." The style continues to be so popular today that it may seem as though the period never ended. With its humble origin, the Colonial interior has come to represent classic American living.

In early Colonial, Cape Cod, and Saltbox homes, there were many design firsts. Understandably, the Colonial-, Cape Cod–, and Saltbox-style interior evolved rapidly during the Colonial era. These interiors relied on a combination of natural materials such as wood, glass, brick, and plaster. At the time, there was little else besides these raw resources available to colonists.

These walls, ceilings, and floors were the early forms for interior finish details. Dirt floors became platforms of hardwood. Ceilings were exposed beams or the underside of the roof. Later, the beams were concealed behind a smooth plaster ceiling, then decorated with moldings, plaster rosettes, and lighting. Simple walls that were the rough inner surface of the exterior cladding became smooth planes that were paneled, plastered, stenciled, painted, or covered in wallpaper.

Early Colonial interiors were bereft of color. The natural materials created a heavily textured look—rough beams, wrought-iron hardware, brick fireplaces and hearths, thick mantels, and coarse, hand-troweled plaster—that was warm but dark. Over time, color was introduced and became a key style element.

◄ Oxblood red made from natural pigments is used in this new dining room to enhance the architectural features of the trim, built-ins, wainscoting, and ceiling beams. ► The plaster in this new home was hand-troweled to re-create the surface texture of true Colonial homes.

▲ Wide pine flooring recovered from salvage yards is used in the hallway of this newly constructed Saltbox.

While there are distinctive features that embody the Colonial style, recognizing how some of the original finish materials were used will give today's homeowners greater insight into what is appropriate for their own renovations.

Foremost in guiding a restoration or renovation or even new-construction project should be where within the Colonial style owners want their homes to be. As we discussed in previous chapters, the early period Colonials were rustic in look. At the other end of the design spectrum are Revival-style Colonials, which reflect a much higher degree of ornament. In between, there is a very comfortable mid-level style, which represents basically what the average person lived with throughout the period.

▶ Beautiful stenciling in complementary reds and greens livens up this simple Colonial living room, including the gun-stock corner post.

When you are selecting interior finish materials such as wallpaper, paint colors, ceiling materials, or floor coverings, stay in keeping with the general architectural design of your residence. Your vintage-style home will benefit from classic design without feeling like it's a museum as you begin to work within its inherent character.

Now, there are many options to choose from in maintaining a historic flair to your home since there are numerous modern sources for finding and purchasing period-appropriate details. Also, taking cues from successfully restored houses when trying to replace lost details in your period home will help you in deciding what is fitting and what works for your lifestyle. It may seem obvious, but what goes into a home is just as important as what is on the outside.

IN HISTORY

Designed to keep rooms as warm as possible during winter, early Colonials and Capes utilized smaller-scaled interiors and closed-off spaces. Finish materials were an extravagance, so they were applied sparingly. Homeowners emphasized their public spaces by adding wall treatments to indicate the family's status and wealth. Wall paneling and painted or stenciled plaster in the parlor (our version of a living room), for example, showed guests the owner's prosperity. Nonpublic rooms, typically in the back of the house, maintained a modest decorative scheme.

Wall Treatments

A significant improvement over wattle and daub applied to insulate interior walls in the earliest Colonial homes, lime plaster and later gypsum plaster provided the most basic finish material. Even as the colonies prospered during the mid-1700s, simple plaster walls were still the most popular decorative choice.

While some homeowners today choose to keep the walls white like those in the earliest Colonials, painted walls and faux-finished walls were just as common. Sponge painting finds its roots as early as the 1700s and remains a popular wall treatment even in today's newer

▲ A close examination of this irregular pargework indicates that it was probably done by hand.

▼ Plaster walls are scored to create diamond patterns in this Connecticut Colonial. Pargework like this was common in England, where it was primarily used on ceilings.

 In new construction, the rough surface texture of hand-troweled plaster was re-created by applying a skim coat over drywall. Once dried, flat white paint was rolled on, then brushed quickly at random.

homes, regardless of style or vintage. Early examples consist of layered paint—usually a base coat with a second hue sponged over it.

Another method of decorating plaster walls involved painting freehand designs in either geometric or curvilinear designs. The handpainted designs adorned ceilings, floors, and walls and were at first irregular and uncontrolled. This led to stenciling, where the painter had more control over the pattern by using cutout patterns and applying the paint with a stiff brush.

Painted murals also adorned the walls. Mural painters traveled from town to town selling their services to city dwellers and country-folk. Scenes of the neighboring countryside included representations of small villages, farms, and seaports depending on the region. Today, these murals are reproduced as wallpaper designs and seen in foyers, dining rooms, and hallways.

We think of wall paneling today as a highly desirable wall finish reserved for the most prominent places in the home, such as the dining room or study. It is interesting to learn that it actually developed as a means to keep out drafts from gaps in exterior clapboarding. Even the way it was designed and installed in the earliest Colonial homes points to its basic function; vertical planks of handplaned lumber with shiplap edges fit tightly together to block out the flow of air. These joints allow the wood to move with changing weather.

Repairing Plaster

Repairing old plaster is and was an overwhelming task. Chemical compounds break down from climate changes and moisture damage. Also, as foundations of old houses settle over time, deep cracks often develop, requiring the special skills of an experienced plasterer. Today, many homeowners choose to cover the old plaster with drywall. And though it's not true to the period, drywall provides a fine base for applying paint, stenciling, faux finishing, and wallpaper.

▲ Vertical wallboard painted in a soft white contrasts with a subtle floral wall-paper in this period-style guest bedroom.

IN HISTORY

Stenciling was a prominent feature of Colonial homes from the early to mid-18th century, since wallpapers were too expensive to be imported and were not fashioned in the colonies until after the Revolution. Patterns were as simple as fruits, birds, leaves, and flowers along with strong geometric designs such as chevrons, checkerboards, and circles. The patterns on walls follow ceiling lines, move around doors, encircle windows, and sometimes appear on floors and ceilings.

The woodwork in this bathroom is adorned with a stencil and wiping stain to give the room Old World charm.

▶ More affordable than wallpaper, stenciling decorated the walls of Colonial homes in rural areas. A pattern cut from stiff paper allowed the artist to precisely reproduce the pattern with accuracy onto the wall using a stiff brush to apply the color.

◀ A subtle tone-on-tone striped wallpaper gives depth and dimension to the walls above the wainscoting in this Colonial Revival entry hall.

► Irregular-width beadboard is run full height in this new Colonial-style home. The green was selected for its historic appeal, as this was a popular color in the first half of the 18th century.

▲ Flat vertical paneling precluded raised-panel, "picture" frame paneling common in later Colonial homes.

Paneling Styles

There's a reason why walls were covered in panels, not solid sheets: Wood moves with the weather. Decorative details at the joint help disguise any gaps during the dry season. Named for its wide use in building the hulls of boats, shiplap is formed by mating two rabbeted edges. Tongue and groove is better at keeping boards flat, and a bead or bevel at the edge hides gaps. Frame and panel, the most "high style" of paneling methods, holds a large center board flat by using a frame made of smaller boards.

► Vertical wall paneling painted in olive green unifies the open stairwell in this newly constructed Saltbox.

▼ Shiplap wallboard is applied horizontally in this new home, complementing the direction of the ceiling beams.

▷ An exceptional example of Colonial wainscoting, this panel, made from a 23½-in. plank, was a black-market item owing to the English monopoly over all mature timber, which was needed for shipbuilding.

▽ Painted woodwork became fashionable in the American colonies in the early 18th century.

▲ Painted woodwork in colonial blue, reproduction light fixtures, and wrought-iron hinges seen on the built-in capture an 18th-century feeling in this bedroom.

◄ The wainscoting is implied in this hallway with a chair rail and two colors of paint—one above and one below.

▼ As the late Colonial period approached with the emerging Georgian style, woodworkers began incorporating classical details into their paneling and millwork designs. The corner cabinet in this mid-18th-century home, with the carved shell motif and delicate dentil molding flanked by fluted pilasters, is of newer construction yet captures authentic period details.

Choosing Paneling

Paneling evolved from the basic need to insulate Colonial homes. The styles range from the very simple and practical to more elaborate designs. Choosing to use vertical-plank paneling, tongue-and-groove paneling, beadboard, or raised panel depends on how rustic or refined you want your house to look. Raised paneling might look best in the dining room, while beadboard is casual enough for the kitchen or bathroom.

▶ In this bathroom, beadboard paneling stops short of the ceiling. Capped with a heavy molding and a wide chair rail, the space can be used for display or storage.

Beadboard

The edge of tongue-and-groove paneling was often enhanced either with a V-groove or a rounded edge called a bead. Beadboard is now available in sheets made of grooved plywood. Since it's thinner (usually ¼ in.) than true tongue-and-groove boards, sheet beadboard makes a good wall covering in areas where the walls are damaged. It can be used as wainscoting with a simple chair rail in a kitchen or as wall paneling in an informal area such as a family room, child's bedroom, or bathroom.

◀ Beadboard wainscoting and tub decking help to unify this quirky bathroom, tucked under the eaves of the attic. Ceiling molding and beadboard balance the extra-wide chair rail. Although hexagonal floor tile was more popular during bathroom designs of the 1920s, it gives this bathroom its old-fashioned charm.

Living History

JOANNE BURROWS AND HER HUSBAND, RICHARD, wanted to personalize their 1850s Cape after purchasing it in a semi-restored condition from previous owners. Learning as much as she could from books on Rufus Porter (1792–1884), a noted painter who traveled throughout New England and the Mid-Atlantic states painting murals, portraits, and silhouettes, Joanne spent a few weeks preparing sketches, which were scaled to fit the area above the wainscoting in the couple's dining room. Using acrylic paint, she created the background, bringing life and color to the scenery. Then she made stencils out of stiff cardboard of reoccurring designs such as trees, animals, and buildings and used them to fill in the details. Next, she handpainted details on the buildings so they looked like the ones in her town.

▲ The Burrows' Cape-style home and barn are depicted in the lower field, while houses of surrounding neighbors spread out toward the horizon.

▼ The stylized New England countryside, here depicted by over-large trees with tall limbs and wispy branches, pays homage to painter Rufus Porter's mural style.

 The soft floral motif of this wallpaper, which became popular with the Colonial Revival style of the late 19th and early 20th centuries, is appropriately scaled to the size of the room.

Wallpaper When and Where

The wallpaper used in 18th-century homes was often block printed or flocked and may not suit the tastes of today's homeowners. Wallpaper was popular in the Colonial Revival era. Patterns from that period blend well with most historic settings, so don't hesitate to use them. The keys are choosing papers that reflect appropriate color schemes and scaling the patterns to the scale of the room. For example, very large patterns can make a small room look busy and crowded. For those interested in historical accuracy, remember that wallpapers were seldom used in dining areas and hallways.

Colonial, Cape, and Saltbox Colors

Naturally pigmented paints found their way into Colonial homes in the early 17th century, and documents show that some homes had paint on the walls, floors, and ceilings. There are a few colors typically called "Colonial"—a range of greens from very yellow-green to deep blue-greens, deep reds, and yellow ochre appealed to early colonists, while a bright medium blue became fashionable after 1720 when the pigment was first imported from Europe. Since the Colonial period lasted so long as a predominate housing type and developing technology created better pigments that led to new colors, selecting interior colors for your vintage home is much easier and more flexible.

Working from a historic color palette may serve as the basis for getting started in your own home. Each color can be adjusted for its value and intensity to achieve just the right balance for your taste and lifestyle in today's homes. Fan decks are organized from the more muted colors to the more intense, showing the range of values for each color on the same paint strip. This is a great way to see how dark or light the color can be pushed while working within a tonal range that is comfortable for you. Historically appropriate olive green may find its way into your home as celadon, a cleaner, lighter, and less saturated yellow-green.

Once a palette is selected, the color choices will be adjusted according to the proportion, layout, and size of each room. For example, Chinese red may be used in the dining room with small accents of the same color in the butler's pantry. Modifying the proportions of how each color is used from room to room unifies the home throughout the interior, keeping the space flowing and connected between adjoining spaces such as the living and dining rooms.

► A fresher, more revived yellow ochre is used in the study of this recently restored 18th-century Colonial home.

◄ In Colonial times, oxblood red was designated to the service areas of the house and kept out of public view.

▲ Historically accurate, this yellow ochre milk paint brings color and dimension to the woodwork in this newly constructed Saltbox-style home.

► A popular color for today's styles, Chinese red became stylish due to an increase in trade with the Far East during the later half of the 18th century.

▼ Interior colors in Colonial homes prior to the introduction of the Georgian style were muddied tones made from natural pigments. Yellow greens, yellow ochre, Colonial blue, and oxblood red were fashionable and first used on trimwork and paneling.

Cozy Colors

While dark colors have a tendency to make rooms look smaller, they can make the room feel more intimate and cozy. In addition, a dark background provides a nice contrast to architectural details if your vintage house has painted woodwork such as doors, trim, and moldings. Also, since natural and artificial lighting affect color in different ways, a dark room can feel light and vibrant in the daytime yet quiet and sophisticated at night under the warmth of incandescent lighting.

Colonial Hues

Color in Colonial homes appeared as early as the 18th century as natural pigments such as iron oxide were mixed with a milk binder and used as paints. These natural pigments yielded a variety of "earth" colors like olive green, yellow ochre, oxblood red, and deep blue. At first, the paint was used on woodwork seen on walls, trim, doors, and boxed ceiling beams, while the wall was left in whitewashed plaster. As the Federal style of Colonial architecture introduced neoclassical influences from England, soft pastels were used on walls, which contrasted against off-white moldings, trim, and woodwork.

The bright green color of the trim surrounding doors and windows is taken from the actual colors used in the dining room at Mount Vernon during the Federal period.

► By painting the deep recesses of the corner cabinet vibrant vermilion, the Colonial blue comes to life in this period home.

▼ In this newly constructed period room, the freshness of white walls against a brighter olive green trim creates a pleasing contrast.

Start Small

When you're ready to choose a paint color, it's important to experiment and to start small. Purchase quarts of the colors that appeal, then test each one. For example, you have your mind made up about a yellow kitchen but aren't sure whether buttercup or sunshine will look better. Test the color on a wall during daylight hours, preferably near a window so you can check the tone in various degrees of natural light and later under artificial light. Also, if you paint your test patch near the window, then you can see how it works with the trim—assuming you're using the same trim color. Remember, a small paint chip from a fan deck may not read the same way when magnified on walls.

▲ Pastel colors found their way into the houses of the late Colonial period as influenced by trends set in the English and French neo-classic styles. This modern interpretation uses a palette of soft gray and pale yellow to enrich the beauty of the architectural period details.

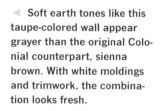 Contrasting paint colors applied to the walls, ceiling, and woodwork intensify the architectural elements in this dining room. The ceiling and wainscot are painted in the same color, divided by the soft white baseboard, chair rail, and ceiling molding. Deep rose walls are made more intense by the complementary green tones.

Soft earth tones like this taupe-colored wall appear grayer than the original Colonial counterpart, sienna brown. With white moldings and trimwork, the combination looks fresh.

▲ Inspired by a color palette from the Federal period, the greens, golds, and off-whites in this modern living room work together to create a dramatic architectural effect. Pale green walls act as an interesting counterpoint to the strong gold on the ceiling and the red on the bookcases, while soft white accentuates wood moldings and trim.

Ceilings

The first Colonial, Cape Cod, and Saltbox homes were small in scale. By the mid-1700s, wealthy individuals who could afford the luxury of building bigger houses did, and soon larger scale was incorporated into the styles.

In the early stages of Colonial building, ceiling heights were low on the first floor while sleeping lofts in the attic spaces of Capes and Saltboxes were vaulted, following the slope of the roofline. Two-storied Colonials had flat ceilings in the sleeping rooms with vaulted ceilings in the attic space, which was often used as a sleeping room and playroom for the children. In all cases, the supporting structures of the ceiling plane were left exposed; large-sized rough-hewn beams in-filled with plaster supported the floor and roof rafters above.

Exposed beam ceilings were common to the style, yet by the mid-18th century, as interiors became more refined and sophisticated, the roughness of the beams were concealed with finished boards called boxed beams. The boxed beams were painted to match the rest of the

▲ Ceiling beams are left exposed in this attic bedroom, emphasizing the slope of the eaves. Insulating plaster kept in its natural, hand-troweled finish gives the room Colonial charm.

▼ The finished beam spanning the length of this bedroom is purely decorative in this newly constructed home.

interior millwork details in the home, and in some regions, such as in Pennsylvania where there was a strong German influence, the beams were stenciled.

As styles increasingly became more classically based during the American Federal period in the late 18th century, the use of plasterwork and plaster moldings appearing in ceiling medallions or crown moldings replaced exposed beams as the new style. Colonial Revival homes of the late 19th and early 20th centuries often incorporated these plasterwork details to maintain more refinement in design than rustic.

▼ A period-inspired chandelier hangs from a ceiling beam in this new Saltbox.

► Wallpaper hung on the walls and ceiling in this hallway accentuates the charming character of the sloping ceiling, while a colorful rag rug warms original chestnut floors.

▼ A bedroom built in the attic space of a vintage Saltbox is a cozy retreat with its low ceiling and angled walls.

Painted floorboards appeared in more rustic Colonial houses as a way to freshen up worn floors and provide a pleasing contrast to the abundance of wood used on walls and ceilings.

 ## The Fifth Plane

Often overlooked but vitally important in the grand scheme of things, the fifth plane—the ceiling hanging above our heads—affects the whole psychology of the enclosing space. Too high and we feel small; too low and we feel confined. Since Colonial architecture used both flat ceilings and vaulted ceilings, the option exists for today's homeowner to have a variety of ceiling heights without sacrificing a historic feeling. Use high ceilings to create a feeling of space and freedom. Lower ceilings suggest warmth, security, and intimacy.

An inspired interpretation of beams combined with tongue-and-groove ceiling and wall paneling gives this kitchen its Colonial flair.

Exposed ceiling beams give this expansive kitchen a rustic feel and add texture to the open plan interior.

Ornamental Beams

To look convincing, "fake" exposed beams should run in the same direction as if they were structural. Take a cue from the existing joists to see which direction to run the beams. If you plan to add overhead lighting in the room, decide on its location before installing the beams. Not only do you want to make sure the location of the light falls correctly in relation to the beams, but also keep in mind that it most likely will be harder to run wiring after the beams have been installed.

A ceiling beam with its mortise notch exposed indicates that it was either reconfigured or recycled from another building. Regardless, it's probably not providing support for the ceiling.

By mid-18th century, exposed rough-hewn ceiling beams fell out of fashion as Colonial prosperity flourished. Here, painted box beams give this bedroom a more refined look.

This new home on Cape Cod hints at the rustic character of old Colonials with its exposed beam ceiling, iron chandelier, and wide plank floorboards.

Floors

The earliest Colonial houses had nothing more than beaten-earth floors, which were often covered with a thin layer of straw in an effort to keep dust down. Later flooring in Colonial, Cape Cod, and Saltbox homes was comprised of pine, chestnut, or oak planks, as available regionally. Wooden floors were seen throughout the main areas of the house. The boards varied in width depending on the type and age of wood and were laid in running lengths. As the supply of old-growth forests diminished, board sizes narrowed.

Today, antique heart pine and reclaimed chestnut are most desirable for hardwood floors. These older-growth woods for the most part possess a highly sought after grain and are denser than younger lumber. Boards from these trees are less prone to dinging and experience less movement because the wood is so hard. As expected, this flooring is expensive because the wood is so scarce.

▼ Floor stenciling like this black-and-white checkerboard pattern simulates the effects of marble flooring seen in English manor houses of the period.

This old-growth eastern white pine floor is shown in a more traditional farmhouse style. Finished with a high-resin tung oil, the resulting warm tone is the reason it's called Pumpkin Pine.

More widely available choices are narrow-strip oak and pine, which, depending on installation methods, will blend in nicely with the period character of Colonial-style homes. Floor boards can be held in place with wooden pegs, reproduction square nails, or fitted together by shiplap or tongue-and-groove edges.

Painted floors frequently found their way into original Colonial-, Cape-, and Saltbox-style homes. The colors brightened up otherwise dark interiors and often matched wall paneling and trims within a room. Stenciled motifs also appeared as decorative borders on finished, raw, and painted floors, depicting fine woven rugs. In some houses, the floors were painted in a faux finish that resembled marble. This continues to work as a solution for heavily worn floors in today's vintage homes.

Rather than leaving a floor bare, floor cloths, an inexpensive alternative to area rugs, were used in the finest and more rustic houses throughout the Colonial period. Coarse canvas primed with animal glue and painted in a variety of freehand or stenciled geometric designs created a warm addition.

Tile, stone, and brick were rarely used in Colonial homes. Most often, brick lined the chimney and fireplace and was used on the hearth because of its inherent fire-resistant qualities. Stone, particularly slate, might be used as a hearth material depending on regional availability.

A simple floorcloth protects the antique pine in this Cape renovation.

▶ Old-growth eastern white pine, with its wider widths, is a rare commodity but can be purchased through salvage companies that mill it into board for flooring.

IN HISTORY

Architectural salvage means big business as historic-minded homeowners look to repair and replace the floors in their vintage-style homes with the real thing. The process of reclaiming wood relies on being in the right place at the right time, as salvage seekers often buy floorboards in bulk lots from homes being torn down all across the country. These "antique" boards demand high prices, depending on the type of wood and patina. Some of the most sought after species include chestnut and heart pine.

▶ Reclaimed from old factories and textile mills along the East Coast, southern longleaf heart pine, with its rich, amber heartwood and its tight, vertical grain, is a harder, denser wood than lumber from younger trees.

◀ Historic charm is captured in this modern-day bathroom through the artistically painted black-and-white checkerboard floor.

▼ Since wall-to-wall carpeting was not used until the Federal styles developed during the late 18th century, floors were covered with simple floor cloths. This one has a geometric design painted on canvas and protected by several coats of varnish.

▶ The distinctive knotholes of old-growth New England pine enhance the beauty of these salvaged floorboards, which are also of irregular widths.

▼ Because of the authentic nature of old-growth eastern white pine, it's appropriate not only in rustic settings but also in more formal or traditional-style Colonial homes like this one. The dark stain evokes a warm, aged feeling.

Game Board

IN THIS MUDROOM, worn-out attic boards get a lift with an up-to-date checkerboard design. First, the homeowners lightly sanded the old boards to loosen dirt and remove old varnish, then they used a roller to give two coats of red latex paint to the prepared surface. Next, using masking tape, they sectioned off the squares set at a 45-degree angle from the wall. Black semigloss latex paint was used to complete the checkerboard effect. Once dry, the entire floor was coated with a clear polyurethane sealer.

The checkerboard design adds character to this tired mudroom floor.

◀ **Both attractive and durable, antique oak offers a rich alternative to pine flooring in any period-style home.**

Old-Fashioned Floors

ARCHITECT AND BUILDER McKie Roth is fascinated with old Colonial and Saltbox homes. He turned his passion for old buildings into a thriving business by building new houses that look old. When Roth built his own home, he took great care in doing things the "old-fashioned way." He chamfered the edges of each pine board before sealing it. In keeping with the original technique, he used reproduction square nails to attach the boards to the floor joists below. The beautiful results are period-inspired yet durable enough for modern living. Since each board is sealed individually with a polyurethane finish, light reflects unevenly across the surface, creating interesting highlights.

Putting in extra time and care, McKie Roth has created a new floor that has all the richness of an antique.

◄ A brick hearth protects the area around the fireplace in this upstairs bedroom.

IN HISTORY

Recycling is not a new concept—in fact, the colonists reused wood, iron, and glass out of necessity as they added on to their buildings. Today, there's a shortage of old-growth lumber, so many turn to "recovered" wood that's cut down and may have been lying on the bottom of an old mill pond, for example. Recovered wood yields wider planks than younger trees. Its unique coloring, a rich, chocolate cherry, attests to its age, which can be from 200 to 500 years old. Recovered lumber, never milled, can be dangerous to plane, though, as nails and other metal objects may be embedded in it.

FOUR

Kitchens, Baths, Storage, and Mudrooms

HEN UPDATING an old house, the first thing most look for is how to find more space. Often, finding enough of it in a Colonial-, Cape-, or Saltbox-style house is a tremendous challenge. Usually adding it—whether in the form of storage or a new room—is first on the renovation wish list. Kitchens, bathrooms, storage, and special spaces like mudrooms are integral to the American family home, but how do homeowners get the room they need without sacrificing the rhythm and scale of the historic style?

One solution is to build a new addition onto the existing structure. Often, this is the simplest way to get that extra area needed to open up a small kitchen, complete a master bedroom, or add another bathroom. Of course, the most direct answer may also be the most expensive—or may just not be feasible given code or landmark districting constraints. The good news is that the general boxy plan of homes from this period makes building on a relatively straightforward proposition. After all, today's homeowners aren't the first to expand these homes. The colonists themselves added on to their homes as their fortunes and families increased, so there's a wonderful tradition of just how these additions should look.

It's also possible to "find" space within the original home. One option to consider is taking down walls between adjoining spaces. This is where bringing in an architect, general contractor, or design professional is helpful. Often, an outside party can easily see where the potential for expansion exists.

◀ **Reproduction hardware was the finishing touch on this custom-made cabinetry with raised panels and spice drawers in this antique Cape kitchen.**
▶ **A new bathroom was added under the eaves of the roof in this old Cape.**

▶ A downstairs parlor, or sitting room, was turned into a reading room after bookcases were added. Requiring only 10 in. of shelf depth, these bookcases hug the wall.

▼ Period details give this new home a Colonial feel while accommodating modern living with its open eating area.

The other choice might be to make space within the nooks and crannies. A modest half bath might be located under a stairwell, for example. Or often there's space for a closet to be built into the corner of a room.

Whatever the solution, it's important to keep in mind that updating an older home to accommodate a modern kitchen and bathrooms, to gain additional closet space, or even to add a mudroom can use up a big portion of the construction budget.

Homeowners should plan very carefully. Before meeting with a professional, it is helpful to have some ideas worked out on paper. Successful renovation projects are those that plan for the entire home, even though only one room may be under renovation at a time. This is the best insurance that there is continuity of the design throughout the house once the project is finished.

Kitchens

Most kitchens in Colonial homes were added when electricity and plumbing were installed. Homeowners often find themselves tearing down old "ells" or remodeling out-of-date designs. Planning a practical, appealing kitchen for you and your family while remaining sensitive to the historic nature of the style involves selecting a combination of textures, colors, cabinetry, hardware, and countertop materials that will fit into the Colonial aesthetic of the rest of the house.

Consider the scale and proportion of the original house—not just ceiling heights and room dimensions but also trim and molding profiles and window openings. Red pine for the living-room floor might be the inspiration for beautiful kitchen cabinetry. Door and window styles should inform the detail on the kitchen cabinetry. Original hardware influences the type of hinges, handles, and pulls selected for cabinet doors and drawers.

▲ This simple frame-and-panel design was inspired by Shaker crafts design. Butcher's wax was layered onto the limestone countertop before it was polished to a high sheen.

▼ A new addition gave the homeowners plenty of kitchen space for preparing meals along with a generous table for informal gatherings. The base cabinets of the work island have a convenient wine rack and storage drawer.

Another design option is to choose nontraditional kitchen components and finish materials. Replacing built-in cabinetry with free-standing furniture or using soapstone countertops and punched-tin door panels will create a rustic Colonial flavor—and work well in a home that already has this early period look. Likewise, cabinetry made from knotty pine, finished oak, maple, or birch, designed with the simplicity of a batten door, can also reflect an early period

◀ Old cabinets spruced up with milk paint are outfitted with pewter bin-pull hardware and glass fronts to create a nostalgic feel.

► Tongue-and-groove paneling was used as a finishing material for the work island and base cabinets in this kitchen renovation. The Sub-Zero® refrigerator is concealed behind wooden panels that match the upper cabinetry.

▼ The casual style of this kitchen is captured by the exposed ceiling beams, a simple shaker rail that stands in for a coat closet, and the kitchen's central work island that doubles as a table for quick meals.

▲ Cabinetry flanking the window above the sink hints at old Colonial style with its open shelving.

Colonial. Wrought-iron hardware in Colonial bean Suffolk, spear Suffolk, or bean-and-spear shapes also lends an authentic look. Butcher-block, slate, or soapstone countertops work well with the design of most Colonial, Cape Cod, or Saltbox kitchens. Oversized farm sinks and hammered-metal sinks with handles or spigot-style faucets are all suitable to the period.

Dishwashers, double ovens, and refrigerators, not to mention blenders, microwaves, and food processors, need to be accessible without being the focal points of the kitchen's décor. Hide them if you prefer, or leave them in plain sight and rely on finish materials to carry the Colonial spirit.

▶ Open shelving, which finds its design roots in the Colonial cupboard, makes putting away dishes much easier after washing.

A Cape Kitchen

EILEEN AND KEN LEAVITT bought their 1808 Cape, which overlooks the Ossipee Mountains in New Hampshire, in 1974. Both loved the style and appreciated the hardships the original owners must have suffered building it. As with most homes nearly 200 years old, the house has gone through many changes. The Leavitts did extensive research in order to restore the house accurately, with Ken doing most of the carpentry. Then, a devastating fire destroyed all their work, and Ken and Eileen had to start over.

▲ A wall-hung cupboard with punched-tin panels conceals the microwave.

▲ The kitchen is large enough to fit a modern range and an antique wood-burning stove.

▲ The door to the food pantry is finished with punched-tin panels, as is the wall-hung cabinet in the main kitchen.

▲ Ken Leavitt designed the kitchen's painted hutch and tall pine cupboard. The hinges, door latches, and turned-wooden knobs are based on interior details elsewhere in the house.

The Leavitts's new addition was constructed from materials recycled from old houses. Avid collectors, they quickly amassed odds and ends from salvage yards, antique shops, and barn sales. The result is an awe-inspiring rebuilt wing that houses a kitchen, breakfast nook, food pantry, and guest bath. It isn't a Williamsburg reproduction, but the Colonial flavor is felt the minute you walk inside. The kitchen, for example, has modern appliances that are concealed behind period cupboards and cabinetry.

▲ Frame-and-panel cabinets were built around this old soapstone sink.

◄ This view from the patio shows the new addition on the right. A new kitchen, pantry, bathroom, and breakfast room occupy the first floor, while the upstairs accommodates a new master bedroom suite.

An old farm table was retrofitted with base cabinets and drawers, creating functional workspace in this eat-in kitchen. Simple Shaker knobs, beadboard paneling, and a distressed wooden countertop contribute to the kitchen's Colonial style.

This island offers additional space for cooking without cluttering the otherwise tight traffic flow of the kitchen.

The keeping room in early Colonial houses was an early example of an eat-in kitchen. Here, the mistress of the home prepared the daily meals on an open hearth, baked bread in a beehive oven, and washed dishes. Families spent much time by the fireplace in the keeping room during the winter.

In the summer, kitchens were moved to an outbuilding near the garden or housed in a lean-to attached to the rear of the house. The invention of the cast-iron cooking stove in the 1700s created the need for a room designated for meal preparation, and the kitchen became a standard addition.

▲ A freestanding sideboard was specially designed with beadboard paneling and reproduction Colonial hardware to separate the eat-in kitchen from the family room.

▶ These black granite countertops in this remodeled 1784 Cape kitchen have a honed finish, which looks like the soapstone used for the sink but is much easier to keep clean because granite is a denser material.

▼ One end of this newly built Saltbox kitchen is devoted to built-in cupboards, providing plenty of storage space for dishes, dry goods, and an overflow supply of pots and pans.

IN HISTORY

Workspaces in Colonial kitchens included a few tables, shelving used as open cupboard space, and an assortment of wooden barrels to store dry goods. It was not until the Victorian era in the late 1800s that kitchens developed into a more sophisticated arrangement of appliances, cabinets, and countertops. Surface materials for countertops were practical; wooden butcher block made cutting meat and vegetables easier without dulling knife blades, while cool marble slabs allowed pastry dough to be rolled out onto the surface without sticking. Natural stone or wood was also commonplace in these kitchens.

▷ A pine vanity dating from the 1850s finds new life as the main kitchen sink in this Colonial-style home.

◁ Painted Shaker-style cabinetries with leaded glass fronts accompany a newly made soapstone sink and countertop.

Colonial Kitchen Made to Order

YOUR KITCHEN DOESN'T HAVE TO LOOK like it belongs in a museum to work with the antique style of your home. How much historical accuracy or character you want for your kitchen is up to you to decide. The owners of this newly built kitchen added the whimsical touch of a delicatessen with a chalkboard menu. The tongue-and-groove paneling on walls and cabinetry, along with exposed ceiling beams and bin-pull hardware, hints at Colonial details, while the clean top cookstove, built-in oven and microwave, and extensive counter space with an additional vegetable sink would be any gourmand's dream.

In addition to the exposed beams, paneling, and hardware, chicken wire on the upper cabinet doors highlights the Colonial style of this kitchen.

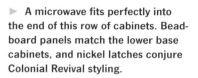 ▶ A microwave fits perfectly into the end of this row of cabinets. Beadboard panels match the lower base cabinets, and nickel latches conjure Colonial Revival styling.

◀ Appliance garages keep toasters, blenders, and mixers handy, while kitchen countertops remain free of clutter.

Sinks and Faucets

Rummaging through salvage yards in pursuit of an old soapstone or enameled iron sink can be fun and pay off in savings. Be sure to check out the fittings and threads of these old treasures, though, to ensure that they meet local plumbing codes and can accommodate modern pipes.

▶ Twin ovens would otherwise look too heavy in this Saltbox kitchen if it weren't for the balancing of a soapstone sink.

▼ A new Saltbox kitchen captures the period's rustic style with the exposed beam ceiling and ochre milk-painted cabinets. Blending in with the appliances, a black soapstone sink creates a visual counterpoint.

Fit for King George

NO DETAIL IS SPARED IN THE DESIGN of this lavish gourmet kitchen. The kitchen features two large clean-up areas: one by the window and the other a work island used for scrubbing vegetables and fruit. Glass-fronted upper cabinets keep the space open with dishes in sight, while lower cabinets outfitted with bin-pull hardware appear as individual pieces of furniture with their raised-feet design. Modern appliances such as the refrigerator are concealed behind wooden panels, while stainless steel double ovens and the dishwasher remain in clear view. An oversized copper hood illuminates the six-burner cooking stove with recessed halogen lights and provides maximum ventilation control.

▼ The stainless steel double ovens and dishwasher are kept in full view, while small cabinets located high above are perfect for storing seasonal dishware.

◄ Two generous work islands keep cooks busy without feeling crowded.

◄ A corner cabinet, not unfamiliar to old Colonial homes, serves as a pantry for the new kitchen.

STYLE *your* WAY

Rustic Charm

KNOTTY PINE CAPTURES THE RUSTIC quality of Southern Colonials in this newly remodeled kitchen without limiting the convenience. Split work surfaces are appropriate for a variety of activities; the raised butcher-block counter is perfect for chopping, while the lower, granite-covered unit makes rolling out pastry dough a much easier task. Open plate racks stand in well for enclosed, overhead cabinets, and a simple shaker peg rail keeps herbs and a hanging spice cabinet within reach.

A variety of textures enhances the rustic charm of this renovated kitchen.

 Simple, unadorned frame-and-panel kitchen cabinetry fits right into this newly built Colonial-style home.

◄ A conveniently placed sash window over the sink allows homeowner Barbara Feller-Roth to look out at her garden while she's working in her kitchen.

Derby Days

Elegant and refined, the Colonial style of the Derby house reflects the prosperity of New Englanders, which was the result of the burgeoning shipping industry. With a little tenacity and a lot of patience, owner and interior designer Cuby Derby and her husband, Dan, ran out the chickens and 12 cats that occupied this charming home and began an extensive restoration project that would take them three years.

Although the main house had most of its original details in place, the Derbys decided to gut the old ell connecting the main house to the barn to put in a new kitchen. Since both like to entertain while they cook, it was important for the Derbys to keep the kitchen as open as possible, while providing enough space to store their cooking utensils.

▲ Space was expanded in the kitchen by adding a bay window, which makes for a cozy place to sit while chatting with the cook.

▲ The wall in the dining room was bumped out to accommodate plumbing for an additional half bath. A built-in cabinet turns a portion of the wall cavity into useable space.

◄ An old-fashioned dry sink provides cupboard space for the overflow of Cuby Derby's blue china collection seen in the adjacent open-shelved hutch.

The original fireplace served as a partial room divider, which was built out on both sides to create valuable pantry space. An existing narrow closet running alongside the flue was outfitted with shelves and served as the baking pantry with a much larger pantry located conveniently nearby.

Taking over space from a hallway connecting the formal parlor to the dining room yielded valuable space for additional cupboards and a small guest bath. Open shelving provided storage accessible from the kitchen, while a small cupboard located directly behind it opened into the adjacent dining room.

Since there was no existing bathroom on the first floor, the reconfigured hallway provided enough room for a small guest bath. Pipes were run through a narrow plumbing chase from the cellar below, with space left over to incorporate ductwork for the heating and air-conditioning system.

▲ The new kitchen takes full advantage of the attic space by opening the ceiling to expose the beams and rafters. A built-out beam houses HVAC ductwork. Custom-designed raised panels conceal the two refrigerators seen in the background.

◀ Narrow closet space running alongside the chimney flue is now a handy pantry.

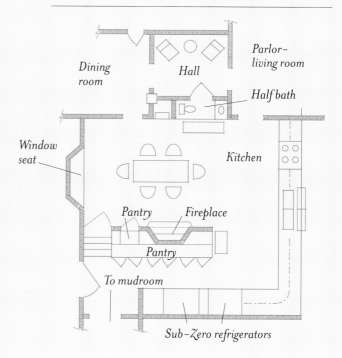

Remodeled Kitchen, Hall, and Bathroom

Dining room

Hall

Parlor-living room

Half bath

Window seat

Kitchen

Pantry

Fireplace

Pantry

To mudroom

Sub-Zero refrigerators

Bathrooms

Since indoor plumbing had yet to be invented in Colonial times, the first bathrooms, those from the Victorian era, are most appropriate for an updated Colonial-, Cape-, or Saltbox-style home. Claw-foot tubs and elaborate pedestal sinks, pristine tiling or decorative wallpapers and paneling all fit in this design. Homeowners with a yen for steam showers, Jacuzzi® tubs, and double sinks shouldn't be discouraged—appropriate models of these options are

▼ Using the space from a spare bedroom, the home-owners were able to build a new master bathroom.

available today and are easily integrated into a home in the Colonial style.

Finding the space to expand a bath or to locate a new one, however, may not be easy. Homeowners often convert an extra bedroom into a bath. And hidden spaces such as the room beneath a front staircase or an unused closet can be outfitted with a toilet and small pedestal sink.

Pedestal sinks, which were used even by the Greeks and Romans, can solve a space problem as well as add to the nostalgic look of a bath. These elegant sinks are so popular that they are still available in a variety of bowl-and-stem designs. Finding one that appeals and is suitable for your Colonial is usually not difficult. The new pedestal sinks are designed with a larger rim to accommodate toothbrush holders, soap dishes, and guest towels. Consider a wall-hung sink, which will work within the period style, for areas where plumbing is tight.

Using a cabinet or dresser and retrofitting it with a sink and faucet is an attractive option. It's one that relates back to the era of commodes—a handsome wooden cabinet with a pitcher and washbasin on top and a single or double door below to hide the chamber pot. Today, this humble look is not only popular but also provides additional storage below.

Vintage claw-foot tubs are plentiful at salvage yards and can be spruced up with an inexpensive refinishing process. Modern tubs complete with Jacuzzi jets can also be found in vintage styles with accompanying faucet designs that reflect old-fashioned hand-held showerheads.

▲ The wall cavity allowed just enough area to build recessed storage niches and a medicine cabinet. The beadboard wainscoting was brought up to the underside of the small window, allowing for additional storage and display space.

▲ There was just enough room under the stairs of this antique Colonial to house a half bath, with the sink placed under the highest point to allow for optimum headroom.

IN HISTORY

In 1785, after his tenure as ambassador to France, Benjamin Franklin brought home to Philadelphia a copper bathtub. In those days, the bathtub was a luxury and few people owned one (or cared to own one). Set in front of a fire for warmth, the tub was filled bucket by bucket with hot water. By the late 1800s, homes were designed with indoor plumbing and new rooms just for bathing.

▶ Wall-hung sinks bring charm to this modestly sized vintage home in the Cape style, while simple hooks offer a place to hang towels.

The wainscoting in this bathroom was bumped out to accommodate plumbing pipes for the sink. The wide-capped molding makes the perfect perch for toiletries.

With additional headroom created by the skylight, the guest bath fits nicely under the eaves.

Closed Quarters

The only place to put a bathroom in this Colonial Revival home built in the late 1870s was in the attic. Carefully laid out, the bathroom worked with the slope of the gable. A small pedestal sink was placed close to the pocket door, where the ceiling was at its highest, six and a half feet. Instead of a conventional shower and shower curtain, homeowner and interior designer Moya McPhail decided on a handheld shower. This worked to keep the room open in feeling. Wall space was fitted with handy towel bars and racks for bath linens; baskets and tub racks made a convenient place to put toiletries.

▲ Homeowner Moya McPhail used a combination of ceramic and reflective glass tiles to jazz up the tight space of the guest bath.

◄ A handheld shower takes up less space than an overhead shower.

▲ Harkening back to a period when freestanding furniture was common, a simple pine cupboard replaces a traditional linen closet in this bathroom.

◀ Beadboard surround dresses up this massive cast-iron soaking tub.

▶ **This little dresser is transformed into a quaint vanity with a little ingenuity and colorful milk paint in a remodeled Colonial home.**

A Perfect Fit

A modestly sized powder bath required some clever thinking to liven up its closetlike proportions. Deep-red wallpaper with tiny gold bees offered an interesting pattern and brought color to the walls, while an antique sewing table presented a whimsical and unexpected alternative to the typical pedestal sink—or even a basin set into a dresser.

Tiny drawers in this sewing table provide handy storage for decorative soaps and hand towels.

▶ Though the old-fashioned claw-foot tub is the focal point in this remodeled bathroom, modern amenities abound, including a steam shower with a glass enclosure, retro light fixtures, and a new linen closet.

▼ No shortage of space in this bathroom renovation as an unused bedroom is transformed into a master bath and dressing area. Set apart from the steam shower, an old-fashioned claw-foot tub takes in spectacular views of the backyard.

▶ A refreshing change from the pedestal sink, this table has been modified to serve as a vanity in a small guest bath.

Architect or Interior Designer?

Architects and interior designers are qualified to handle interior construction projects. Both can prepare drawings and provide specifications in order to procure bids from contractors. But how do you know when you need one more than the other? If your home requires structural changes, as in building a new addition, you should hire an architect to prepare the drawings. Interior designers are trained to work with the nonstructural interior issues such as space planning and selection of interior finish materials, furnishings, and final decorative accessories.

In most cases, the architect or designer can hire the contractor and oversee the construction process. You can find an architect or interior designer with expertise in Colonial-, Cape Cod–, and Saltbox-style homes by contacting these professional organizations: the American Institute of Architects, the American Society of Interior Designers, and the International Interior Design Association.

▲ Storage doesn't have
to be built-in to be incon-
spicuous. Here, a rustic cupboard for linens, painted in
muted yellow, was built on
an upstairs landing outside
the bathroom door.

◀ A new Saltbox has old-
fashioned style with its
small powder room located
off the main hallway. A
raised-basin sink with
spigot- style faucet pairs
with a water-pitcher acces-
sory and sits on a wooden
cabinet, resembling an
antique commode.

Storage

In Colonial times, built-in storage was not in abundance. Often limited to a closet tucked neatly alongside the chimney flue or a corner cupboard in the living or dining room, storage wasn't needed as it is today. While built-in cabinets during the Colonial period displayed the family's collection of export china, we rely on them to hide computers and televisions.

Adding closet space in older homes is a difficult task since the options are limited. But room for closets can be accommodated without sacrificing valuable space. For example, built-out closets

▼ Before closets, cabinets, or other types of built-ins, Colonial homes used open shelving called "cup boards" for storing their household wares.

▲ A corner cabinet in this new Federal-style kitchen is the perfect showcase for the homeowner's earthenware and pewter collections.

strategically placed between doors or flanking a central window only require about two feet of depth. Another way to get the most space out of a small area is by maximizing the vertical space within. Using the many types of closet organizers, you can create essential storage space from smaller areas.

Window seats were found in Colonial homes dating back to the 18th century. With them, homeowners gained additional storage without furniture (which was expensive and not yet mass-produced). A window seat also provided an extra seat in the room. A hinged lid made for easy access to the storage area below that blended in design and detailing with the room's wainscoting.

The doors on this new master-bedroom closet were bench-built, imitating the rhythm of other doors upstairs. Crown molding was added to unify the space.

Today's homeowners have realized how practical window seats really are, from providing a cozy little space to curl up and read to offering out-of-the-way storage for those items only used a few times a year. Outfitted with a raised-panel front and strap hinges, window seats have a timeless quality and efficiency that fit into almost every room in the house.

Bookshelves are the least intrusive type of storage units, whether they are built floor to ceiling or simply run along a perimeter wall under the chair rail. The depth of each shelf need only be 10 in. to accommodate most books and can be used to store CD and DVD collections without difficulty.

IN HISTORY

The British crown imposed taxes on the American colonists in a number of ways; the tea tax (remember the Boston Tea Party?) is just one example. England also imposed a tax on every room in a Colonial home no matter how small— including closets. After the United States won its independence, Federal-style Colonial homes proudly featured more closet space.

► Space under this staircase serves as a convenient coat closet, with its proximity to the front door.

▲ In a new addition off of the dining room of this 1812 Federal-style home, the
fireplace wall was extended to incorporate a much-needed pantry for the kitchen.

▶ The owner of this elegant Revival-style home took a different approach to creating an entertainment cabinet, modifying an American Empire-style sideboard for her television.

▶ The front panel of the sideboard raises and retracts to give clear view to the TV and storage area below.

The view of the long, narrow room in this Colonial farmhouse was opened up to the patio and beyond with the addition of French doors. Built-out bookcases are capped in perfect proportion with the trim on the center doors.

This home in Bath, Maine, uses custom-fitted bookcases to maximize the space in the living room. Along with family photos and artwork, several volumes grace the 10-in.-deep shelving.

Better Guest Relations

INTERIOR DESIGNER NANCY FAYE GLASS didn't need a full-time guest room in her early 18th century Colonial home, so she decided to turn the bedroom adjacent to her master bathroom into a dressing area for her husband. The room now serves double duty as an antique daybed accommodates overnight guests when the need arises, while a small chest of drawers and ample closet space give husband Don Ross plenty of room for his clothes.

Additional closet space in this old Colonial home is solved without sacrificing space. Closets were built 2 ft. out from the room's interior wall, leaving just enough room for a daybed, small chest of drawers, and chair.

New floor-to-ceiling bookcases created just enough space for window seats when this addition was built.

An old Cape built in the 1790s benefits from a cozy reading room created in the living room with the addition of bookshelves.

Mudrooms and More

Finding room for "special spaces," such as a home office, often requires thinking creatively about the existing floor plan. Usually these are planned when remodeling or adding on a new kitchen. Manufacturers of cabinetry offer solutions on how to incorporate a home workspace as part of the kitchen. Component options ranging from fold-down work surfaces to file drawers and mail sorters that match cabinet details and hardware styles make these work centers a seamless part of the kitchen.

Living in a Colonial doesn't mean homeowners have to give up big-screen televisions and surround-sound systems. There are attractive built-ins or freestanding cabinets available. Built-in entertainment units with retractable doors work well and hide equipment. Units with glass fronts will allow an infrared signal to operate CD players and stereo receivers. Door designs, whether glass paneled or not, should be based on existing doors or wall paneling found in the original house for smooth integration with the home's interior.

Having a mudroom is also a nice "extra" and can usually be carved out of an existing entryway. Not only are they the ideal place to remove and store coats, hats, shoes, and boots, but if planned efficiently, they also provide valuable storage space for kids' backpacks, golf clubs, and recycling bins. Creating a mudroom doesn't necessarily require a new addition. If the front door opens directly into the living room, use a durable rug or jute matting to protect the floor. Placing a small bench with a hinged seat in the entryway provides space to store shoes, umbrellas, gloves, and hats. A peg rail, commonly called a shaker rail, also works well.

▼ Today's popular home entertainment systems don't have to dominate the interior of a vintage-style home. The front-panel design on these retractable doors was copied from an existing door in the room. The cabinet hides media components and surround-sound speakers.

When the new laundry room and home office were built, a door opening had to be cut for access. This new addition also provided room for a recessed television and surround-sound components, so the original plane remained intact along the fireplace wall.

STYLE *your* WAY

A small closet keeps coats and boots convenient but out of the way in this newly built mudroom. A durable quarry tile floor laid on the diagonal visually expands the modest space.

Barn Raising

INSTEAD OF BUILDING A NEW ADDITION, the homeowners of a 1790s Colonial decided to maximize the space of an old barn by connecting it to the main house with an enclosed breezeway and converting it into a media and family room.

A hayloft was removed, and the support beams were raised from their original placement 6 ft. off the ground to 9½ ft., allowing adequate head clearance. Two large barn doors were removed, and French doors were put in their place. The muntin design in the French doors mimics the home's six-over-six double-hung sash windows seen next to the new stone fireplace. Rather than traditional flooring materials, the owners decided on a poured-concrete floor. Instead of using running lengths of hardwood flooring, the couple stained and polished the concrete slab.

A converted barn now serves as the family and media room in this late 18th-century Colonial home. Ceiling beams were raised to allow for headroom.

▲ Local fieldstone gives the fireplace rustic charm in this newly built family room.

◀ An armoire cleverly hides the family computer when not being used in this sitting room.

Adding a Mudroom

When faced with having to add a much-needed mudroom to their Colonial-style house that already had two additions—the first built in 1708 and the second added around 1830—Nancy Faye Glass and her husband, Don Ross, weren't quite sure what to do. Taking ideas from the surrounding Merrimack Valley, Massachusetts, farms and old estates in their neighborhood, they decided to add a lean-to. The finished mudroom connected what used to be an exterior door to the 18th-century parlor to a separate outside door leading into the kitchen housed in the early 19th-century addition.

Nancy Faye, an experienced interior designer, took full advantage of the sloping cat's-slide roof by putting in

◀ This view from the kitchen to the mudroom shows the original exterior window and door, which were kept intact to maximize the amount of natural light coming into the room.

◄ A new mudroom with its cat's-slide roof connects the older, 18th-century house with the newer one built in the early 19th century.

a skylight. Keeping the kitchen's original exterior windows and glazed door in place brought in light from the skylight. Complementing the exposed summer beam in the kitchen, she decided to use rough-hewn beams from an architectural salvage yard to create a horizontal ceiling line. This took attention away from the sloped ceiling and redirected the focal point to the interior details.

Nancy Faye designed the mudroom's interior with a window seat mimicking one found in the dining room. She flanked the window seat with two narrow closets and designed the doors after ones found in the 1708 addition. The many hearths that appear in the home inspired the brick floor.

◄ The new mudroom is practical: The built-in window seat provides the perfect place to sit while removing shoes. Its hinged seat allows easy access to storage beneath and conceals HVAC ductwork. A brick floor handles the wear and tear of heavy traffic.

The Best of Both Worlds

THE HOMEOWNERS OPTED TO MIX the nostalgia for old wardrobe closets with newer, more practical closets when they added on to their 1790 Cape to accommodate a new master suite. While the armoire adds elegant charm to the room, built-in closets pay close attention to the fine detailing reflected in the home's architecture.

▲ Built-in closets are set in threes, breaking up the rhythm of a long wall between the bedroom and bathroom doors. Each closet is sized according to either long or short hanging clothes, while the larger, centralized closet is fitted with drawers.

◄ A family heirloom armoire graces the sitting area of this newly built master suite.

▲ When the homeowners of this Cape connected the main house with the barn, they turned the enclosure into a mudroom. The floor, which gets especially hard use in the winter, is protected by a reproduction oilcloth. Closets, antique chests, and cupboards keep everything from garments to gardening tools handy.

◄ Here, a kitchen work center captures the charm of Colonial-style cabinetry with its open shelves and beadboard backing, wooden work surface, and chicken-wire front overhead cabinets.

FIVE

Today's Classic Interior

OVING AND LIVING in a Colonial house doesn't mean having to put up with a cold or hot or darkly lighted house. Even though Colonial-, Cape Cod–, and Saltbox-style homes date back to the early 1700s, they should be as easy and comfortable to live in as houses with all the modern convenience of the 21st century. These homes have survived through the decades—they embody the idea of keeping up with the times. We're introduced to new improvements every day, but think of the colonists who started with so little, then acquired wealth and possessions rapidly as the nation grew and succeeded. They were updating their homes all the time.

This chapter will look at the fireplace—once at the heart of heating and cooking operations in the Colonial home but now transformed into more of a decorative element—as well as other home essentials that we may take for granted: heating, cooling, and lighting. Of course, most period homes were updated as heating, plumbing, and electricity became available. Often, though, such improvements are now outdated, not having been replaced since they were first installed.

At the turn of the 20th century, keeping a house warm was not a difficult problem—just labor-intensive and messy. Of course, in southern climates, heating by a wood-burning fireplace or small gas-burning stove was adequate to take the chill away on a cold night. In the Northeast, this would be insufficient for the extreme winters. For homes in these regions, either gas- or oil-fired boilers that fed hot water to radiators heated the house.

◁ In Colonial homes, the fireplace was the center of family life, providing a source for cooking, heating, and lighting. ▶ A kerosene lantern with hurricane shade has been converted to an appropriately styled electrical light fixture in this vintage Cape.

The advent of electricity brought about some low-tech methods for cooling off, like this ceiling fan with period light fixture.

ELECTRICITY

Candle power lighted Colonials when needed. The first homes wired for electricity employed knob-and-tube wiring and fuse boxes. And though homeowners may think this is a quaint setup, it rarely provides adequate amperage to power a home today. And often it is not safe.

In our time, we run far more electrical devices than were available when many of these homes were electrified, and things we take for granted today—such as air-conditioning—were not widespread until the 1960s. In addition, the electric light bulb was so new when wiring was brought into these old homes that many light fixtures were converted from gas powered to electric powered instead of being replaced entirely.

By updating your home's heating system, adding an air-conditioning system, and investing in the complete rewiring of your house, not only is your Colonial, Cape Cod, or Saltbox home more comfortable, but also more reliable. And there are many ways to faithfully incorporate these modern advances without ruining the style of the home. This chapter offers solutions for integrating these modern conveniences into vintage-style homes without disrupting the historic flavor.

New and old systems such as a high velocity air-conditioning system and a still functioning forced-hot-water radiator make this 1830 Colonial home much more comfortable to live in.

Discreetly hidden behind a hinged wall panel, the circuit breaker box is conveniently accessible from the breakfast room in this 1760s Cape.

Even in today's homes, the fireplace provides warmth and atmosphere, while remaining a strong center for family gatherings.

Fireplaces

Once integral to the function of the Colonial home, fireplaces are today an important part of the design, from the earliest examples built at Jamestown and Plymouth to the grand Colonial Revivals of the 19th century. No longer just a cooking hearth or a source of heat, fireplaces became the source of ambiance for a room and were designed in context with the architectural elements used within the home. Fitted with ornate mantel designs, they presented yet another opportunity for homeowners to display their wealth.

The chimney flue, hearth, and enclosing firebox were constructed from noncombustible materials such as brick or stone, while the surround was typically made of wood and later sometimes tile. The styling of the wood surround varied depending on the adjoining wall treatment.

In early examples of Colonial houses, the fireplace wall was covered with paneling that stretched from floor to ceiling and was often used here instead of white plaster because it was easier to keep clean

A dining-room fireplace dating from 1810 shows a simple mantel design, separate from the surrounding trim. Its profile, as well as the profile of the surround, follows the delicate form of the room's crown molding.

Current fire codes require new fireplaces to have a minimum of 6 in. of noncombustible material between the opening of the firebox and the wooden mantel. The distance between the firebox and the mantel is determined by local or state regulations.

Dinner by the Fire

ARCHITECT McKIE ROTH BUILT HIS REPUTATION
on designing period homes so authentic that they require
a second look. He pays close attention to the finest
details, even those not obvious to the casual observer.
In designing a corner fireplace for the dining room in his
own home in Maine, McKie chose to use reproduction
brick that was of the same dimension as brick used in
the early 1800s, which is smaller than what's common
today. A keen observer will notice the thinness of the
reproduction brick in the coursing of the firebox. McKie
continued the brick from the firebox to the surround,
ensuring a sufficient fireproof barrier before adding the
wooden mantel.

▲ This new fireplace complies with
local building codes—the coursing of
the brick extends from the firebox to
the surround.

◄ Reproduction brick is used on the
surround and the hearth, where, laid
face-side up, it appears wider.

Vertical-plank wall covering provides a protective background from soot buildup from this fireplace. The fireplace mantel is a simple cornice with a plain frieze, while slender pilasters project from the surround.

A decorative detail fills the space between side pilaster and mantel.

of soot. Over time, the fireplace developed its own identity as a stand-alone feature along living-room and sitting-room walls.

Deemed more elegant, moldings appearing as trim on ceilings, baseboards, and chair rails eventually replaced full paneling as the Georgian style emerged in the 1760s. Then, the design of the fireplace became more integrated with the architectural trim; crown moldings with projecting cornices translated as mantels, and trimwork followed the lines of the surround. And as classical motifs were introduced into the design of these Georgian Colonials, fireplace detailing was enriched with dentil moldings and pilasters with decorative capitals.

◀ The decorative carving on this mantel reflects classical detailing with its reed architrave, dentil molding, and fluted pilaster. Classical designs like these are more suitably seen in Georgian, Federal, or Colonial Revival interiors.

This new mantel was replicated from an original 1810 design used in the formal living room. An unusual ovoid frieze panel separates the mantel from the fireplace opening.

▼ Appropriately styled for a Colonial home, this 4-in. mantel is made from a combination of simple moldings set against shiplap wall paneling.

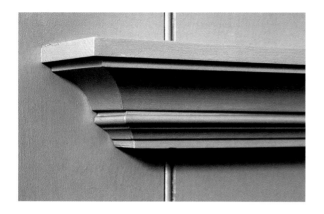

The Evolution of the Mantelpiece

In early Colonial one-room homes, the fireplace served both as a heat source and cooking area. Even when homes expanded and there were multiple fireplaces in the house, the hearth area maintained its prominence. As a source of heat, the fireplace was a gathering place for family and friends and the natural focal point of the room.

Early fireplaces used for cooking often had hooks above the firebox for holding pots and cooking implements. As homes became more refined, a simple shelf mounted above the fireplace to hold prize plates or pewter was added, increasing the utility of the fireplace and its visual interest. Simple moldings eventually became more elaborate. Side supports under the mantel, also decorated with moldings and sometimes columns, completed the surround, making it a three-sided case with a shelf at the top. In the late 1700s, as the number of local craftsmen increased and homeowners grew wealthier, carvings in classical motifs decorated both the top and sides under the shelf.

This section drawing of a molding profile taken from a mantel in a house built in 1810 shows how elaborate designs had become.

▲ A newly built fireplace incorporates features taken from
the original 1830s home.

In with the Old

THIS NEW HOME captures all the ambiance of an early Colonial with its rustic beamed ceiling and oversized fireplace. The fireplace recalls an old-fashioned cooking hearth with its wrought-iron kettle arm and rough beam mantel shelf, although the homeowners opted to use newer variegated brick instead of less-colorful reproduction brick.

The cozy style of the early Colonial makes it a popular choice, even for a new home.

▶ The fireplace and hearth in this new home was inspired by early Colonial examples with its oversized firebox and bee-hive oven. The beehive oven is actually a storage cabinet for wood and kindling.

▼ This new design is suitable for a variety of Colonial homes from the more basic Cape to the Federal styles in rural areas. Its uncomplicated design features a simple cornice, unadorned frieze, and plain pilasters.

Colonial Comfort

As technology improved in the early 1900s, old Colonial homes were retrofitted with heating systems that proved to be quite comfortable. Located in the cellar, boilers heated water that ran through pipes to radiators, either as hot water or steam. A cast-iron radiator, sized according to the dimensions of the room, was a most efficient means of distributing warmth. Radiators have held up well over time and even in today's homes, the originals still function well. Today the boilers, however, often need to be replaced for safety or energy-efficiency reasons.

Although air-conditioning was first introduced in the 1920s, it was unheard of in modern homes until the mid-20th century.

▼ Using boiler-fed forced-hot-water or steam radiators was a standard way of heating Colonial homes during the later part of the 19th century. The cast-iron radiators are still desirable by some homeowners and are an effective source of heat distribution.

◀ The grill covering a heat vent is concealed beneath the window seat in this Colonial Revival home.

▼ Radiator covers were designed to look like a piece of furniture. This example has an open screen front to allow the heat to radiate into the room.

These days, homeowners can install forced-air systems capable of delivering both hot and cool air in conjunction with their old radiators if they don't want to replace them entirely.

Having a comfortable home doesn't necessarily mean tearing into old plaster. Ductwork made from sheet metal or small, flexible plastic tubing can be concealed in vertically stacked closets, inconspicuously dropped ceilings, or run up from the basement through floor cavities.

High-velocity systems are a newer form of climate control, and like many cutting-edge products, cost more than older systems. These all-air systems powerfully deliver hot or cold air through plastic flexible tubing as small as 3 in. in diameter. The small-gauge tubing can be bent in and around tight areas, behind walls, inside closets, or run into the ceiling from attic space above.

Cool Comfort, By Design

When interior designer Moya McPhail updated her 1862 home, one of the most important considerations was updating the heating and air-conditioning system. Within her old lath and plaster walls, there weren't adequate wall cavities to run ductwork through, so she came up with another plan. The location of the dining room provided the perfect solution. The boiler and air-handling system in the cellar was vented up to the second floor through duct chases in an old closet in the dining room. The additional casing for this ductwork created a niche that was perfect for the dining-room sideboard. The result looks as if it was part of the home's original design.

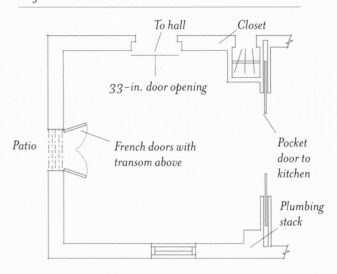

Before

To hall   Closet

33-in. door opening

Patio   *French doors with transom above*

Pocket door to kitchen

Plumbing stack

A low-tech way of bringing in cool breezes from the central hallway, this 19th-century dining room was remodeled to accommodate a transom window that opens and closes above the sideboard. The walls on either side accommodate the home's HVAC ductwork.

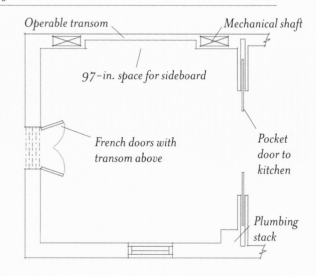

After

Operable transom   *Mechanical shaft*

97-in. space for sideboard

French doors with transom above

Pocket door to kitchen

Plumbing stack

▲ An old floor vent now serves as a supply vent for a new central air and heating system located in the cellar.

◀ Baseboard heating units as seen in this hallway and running along the perimeter wall of the bedroom offer radiant heating without the size and mass of old-fashioned radiators.

Lighting

We have all heard the story about Abraham Lincoln studying his law books by the dim light of a lantern. If he'd wanted better lighting, say by incandescent bulb, he'd have had to wait some 40 years. Most houses built in the mid-19th century relied on gaslights for illuminating the interiors. Only a few of the grand Victorian homes had electricity and only for those owners who could afford it.

Even in the early days of electrical lighting, the design of fixtures varied from a simple, exposed bulb hanging by its electrical wire to a basic porcelain fixture mounted on the wall. As people realized the possibilities for lighting, glass shades were designed to cover the bulb, which eliminated glare and helped diffuse the light into the room.

When homeowners choose light fixtures for their Colonial, Cape, or Saltbox homes, they should keep in mind that the most important consideration is to make a selection that ties in to the inherent design

▲ Wall sconces were usually grouped in pairs hung from a wrought-iron nail in Colonial homes. This design is tall and slender to allow for the slow burning of a candle taper and was made from polished tin or pewter.

◄ The main dining room in this 18th-century half Cape keeps most of its original features with the addition of a reproduction chandelier. Its simple design features candlestick lights with candle bulbs.

◀ These wall sconces are made from tin that has been chemically aged to look old. The candlelike lights and candle bulbs complete the rustic look of the fixture.

▼ This Saltbox has a lantern-type wall light with an anodized aluminum frame and seed glass shade. The coach lanterns hung outside of taverns and ordinaries during Colonial days inspires its design.

of the architecture. A crystal chandelier would be out of place within a home with exposed ceiling beams or board-and-batten doors; one made from iron, tin, or pewter is more in character.

More rustic interpretations of the Colonial style call for lighting fixtures that evoke an earlier period in time, one where candles provided the only source of light. Back then, reflective holders were necessary to distribute the light throughout the room. Other holders were made from wrought iron, forged into chandeliers and sconces by local blacksmiths.

The finer Colonial styles like Georgian and Federal houses may require more stylized fixtures. These grand homes often featured crystal chandeliers imported from Europe, while others were accessorized with plainer glass hurricane-type lamps.

Iron, Pewter, Tin

If your vintage home has been stripped of its light fixtures, deciding what to replace them with may be challenging. While there are many modern styles to choose from, selecting a fixture that is most appropriate to the home's architecture is important. If your home is more rustic, fixtures made from iron, pewter, or tin follow the character of the style. More classically influenced Colonials may incorporate fixtures made from brass, cut glass, or fixtures with hurricane shades.

◄ A more refined example of Colonial lighting, this reproduction fixture allows the lamp to move up and down a pewter rod, easily adjusting the height of the light source. The shade is a later addition to earlier Colonial lighting and directs the light downward for reading.

◄ Colonial lighting relied on candle power and reflective materials for distributing light throughout the room. This reproduction fixture is based on tin wall sconces often made by women.

◄ The clamshell motif on this reproduction light fixture mimics the same detail found on most built-in corner cabinets from the same period.

▲ Called a hall tavern kitchen sconce, this reproduction with its large sized mirror glass was in style in the American colonies as early as 1730. The mirror facets reflect light back into the room.

IN HISTORY

Before gas lighting was a common amenity, people planned their activities more closely to the timing of natural light. During the short days of fall and winter, some artificial light was needed so chores could be completed. The ambient light of the fireplace was supplemented by candles. But candles weren't always a cheap, widely available commodity. Candle making required a good deal of labor, whether it was recovering wax from beehives or forming them from animal tallow. The time-consuming process included melting the wax over large pots and dipping or molding the tapers.

Wrought-iron chandeliers were designed with taper holders and hanging bars that maximized airflow around the fixture, increasing drafts to keep the flames bright, intensifying illumination. This example is well over 150 years old.

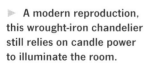 Delicate petals fashioned from iron originally held candles in this reproduction chandelier with New England origins. The wooden baluster-shaped shaft was rare for light fixtures in the late 18th century.

▲ The double-cone design of this chandelier made from tin still operates on candle power as it first did when popular from 1830 until about 1860.

► A modern reproduction, this wrought-iron chandelier still relies on candle power to illuminate the room.

▼ Another rare chandelier from 1790 to about 1830 is available in reproduction. A wood-turned center post supports wrought-iron arms featuring small wooden pears.

▲ An unusual design yet practical in function, this tavern chandelier made from tin uses reflectors mounted behind the shaped arms of the candleholders (now electrified in this reproduction) to cast more light into the room.

IN HISTORY

Chandeliers are an early form of task lighting, used as we do so now to illuminate a table area. People gathered at the Colonial table for more than just meals, so it made good sense to better illuminate this area than other parts of the house. Combining the power of several candles suspended from above increased the ambient light in the room as well. The distance between individual candles and how far they were hung from the ceiling was calculated to produce even burning. The earliest chandeliers have wooden spindles at the center with metal arms that extend in a radial pattern and have metal candleholders that are fitted with dishes to catch wax.

Replacements

There are several options for replacing light fixtures in your period-style home, including searching through antique lighting stores and salvage yards, bidding in online auctions, and buying new reproduction fixtures that are available in historically inspired styles. For a new kitchen, family room, or addition where the historic nature of the house may only be hinted at, new fixtures loosely based on old designs are usually more appropriate.

This reproduction wall sconce has a delicate hurricane glass shade.

▲ This nineteenth century pendant lamp is an early improvement over a bulb hanging by a bare wire.

▲ A reproduction brass chandelier with hurricane glass shades hangs over the dining table in this 1810 Federal home.

IN HISTORY

In the Colonial period, wall-hung lighting was used to
illuminate an indoor area. Lanterns were suspended from
pegs or hooks, or wall sconces were lit. A candle against the
wall threw relatively little light, but once a reflector was
added behind the candle, the amount of light increased
considerably. Round sconces were popular in the early
colonies. They were usually made from tin or, in rarer
instances, copper or brass, which was polished to reflect
light. Later, mirrored glass was used for the same purpose.

Resources

ARCHITECTS, INTERIOR DESIGNERS, AND CRAFTSMEN

Austin Patterson Disston Architects, LLC
376 Pequot Avenue, P. O. Box 61
Southport, CT 06890
www.apdarchitects.com

Brookfield Custom Building
Terrence Colligan
1 Pinewood Road
Brookfield, NH 03872
(603) 522-6718

J. Covington Interior Design
436 Governor Wentworth Highway
Melvin Village, NH 03850
(603) 544-3666

Gerald Cowart, AIA
107 East Gordon Street
Savannah, GA 31401
www.cowartgroup.com

Davitt Design Build
4 Frank Avenue
West Kingston, RI 02892
(401) 792-9799

Nancy Faye Glass
Glass House Design
18 Stevens Street
North Andover, MA 01845
(978) 688-3545

Lynn Hopkins Architect
45 Munroe Road
Lexington, MA 02421
(781) 863-2585

Peter LaBau
The Classic Group, Inc.
420 Bedford Street
Lexington, MA 02420
(781) 761-1200
www.theclassicgroup.net

Moya McPhail Design
Read House, 20 King Street
Port Hope, Ontario, L1A 2R4
Canada
(905) 885-1567
www.eagle.ca/~moya/mail.html

McKie Roth Design
P. O. Box 31
Castine, ME 04421
www.mckieroth.com

Douglas Small
Waterbury Design Associates
818 East Baltimore Pike
Kennett Square, PA 19348
www.waterburydesign.com

Barry Svigals
Svigals + Partners, LLP
84 Orange Street
New Haven, CT 06510
www.svigals.com

Tom Vermeland
Vermeland Architects
4343 Penfield Avenue South
Afton, MN 55001
vermelandarchitects@msn.com

SUPPLIERS

Carlisle Wide Plank Floors
1676 Route 9
Stoddard, NH 03464
www.wideplankflooring.com

C. James Frasier, Artist
Woodstock, VT
(802) 457-1937

Crown Point Cabinetry
153 Charlestown Road
Claremont, NH 03743
www.crown-point.com

Goodwin Heart Pine Company
106 SW 109th Place
Micanopy, FL 32667-9442
www.heartpine.com

The Kennebec Company
1 Front Street
Bath, ME 04530
www.kennebeccompany.com

Period Lighting Fixtures, Inc.
167 River Road
Clarksburg, MA 01247
(800) 828-6990

Rejuvenation
2550 NW Nicolai Street
Portland, OR 97210
www.rejuvenation.com

Sherwin-Williams
www.sherwin-williams.com

Wood-Mode Fine Custom Cabinetry
www.wood-mode.com

Glossary

Baluster A support for the handrail on staircases; also any turned-vase or urn-shaped support.

Bench-built Referring to an item handmade on site, the design of which has been customized based on (usually) space limitations.

Board and batten Typical construction for early Colonial doors and shutters. Wide boards are held in place with thin wood strips called battens.

Boxed beams The furring out of rough-hewn timbers used as support beams in early Colonial homes.

Capital The uppermost decorative part of a column or pilaster.

Cat's-slide roof The longer side of a gabled roof, usually connecting a lean-to with an existing gable.

Christian cross door A four-panel door where the separating members form the shape of an inverted cross.

Clapboard Wooden boards cut with a slight wedge shape used as exterior cladding on Colonial homes.

Cornice The uppermost molding that forms the entablature in architecture.

Dentil molding A classically based motif appearing as square blocks running the length of a molding.

Dormers Windows that project from an attic space or roofline.

Entablature The uppermost section of a building or case good. In architectural terms, an entablature consists of a cornice, frieze, and architrave.

Fluting Thin grooves cut lengthwise in the shaft of a column or pilaster. Also seen as a running design in the frieze area of the entablature.

Frieze A broad, flat section located under the cornice of an entablature.

Gable A steeply pitched roof. The side of the gable forms an inverted V.

Gambrel A pitched roof having a slight interruption of slope.

Handplaning A method of trimming and smoothing timber planks used in millwork construction.

Heartwood The oldest growth of a tree; especially desirable for its density when used as a flooring material.

Honed granite Granite that is polished to a matte finish.

Keeping room In Colonial days, the kitchen.

Leaded glass Glass held in place with lead banding.

Lintel A horizontal, wide molding positioned over doors and windows.

Louvered shutters Shutters made from thin slats of overlapping wood.

Low-hipped (as in roof) A low, hugging roofline usually flat on top with a slight pitch to the sides and front.

Milk paint Natural pigment mixed with lye and a milk product, which acts as a binder for paint.

Muntins Thin wooden strips used to hold glass in its place in doors and windows. The muntins create a definitive grid pattern.

Newel post The end support of a banister on a staircase. The newel post acts as the structural support for the handrail along with the balusters.

Parlor In Colonial homes, the living room.

Pediment A triangular or scrolled top piece to doors, windows, and/or built-in cupboards and cabinets.

Pigment The coloring used for paints. In Colonial times, pigments were taken from nature; iron oxide, lead, and ochre to name a few.

Pilasters Flattened columns used as an architectural enhancement to door trim, mantel designs, and built-ins.

Plinth The lower block on a pilaster, which acts as a base.

Ridgepole The uppermost support of a gabled roof where the rafters connect to create the pitch.

Sidelights Fixed glass panels appearing alongside the front or main door of a Colonial house.

Stringer The notched facing of a staircase that supports the treads and risers.

Transom An overhead glass panel placed above doors that usually swings open for ventilation.

Wattle and daub Plaster (or dung) and straw or small sticks used as an early form of insulation in Colonial homes.

Winder A type of staircase that has one or more turns.

Index

Photo Credits

CHAPTER ONE: What Style Is Your Home?

pp. 4, 5, 14, 18, 21, 22 © Joseph St. Pierre; p. 6 (top) by Scott Gibson, courtesy of *Fine Homebuilding*, © The Taunton Press, Inc.; p. 10 (top) © www.davidduncanlivingston.com; pp. 10 (bottom), 12 (top) © www.carolynbates.com; p. 13 McKie Roth Designs © Randy O'Rourke; p. 15 © Grey Crawford

CHAPTER TWO: Woodwork

pp. 31, 48 (right), 52 (bottom right), 53 © Joseph St. Pierre; p. 35 (bottom) by Kevin Ireton, courtesy of *Fine Homebuilding*, © The Taunton Press, Inc.; pp. 36 (bottom), 37 (bottom), 50 (top & bottom), 54 (top), 66 (top), 69 (bottom), 71 (bottom) © Grey Crawford; pp. 39 (bottom), 43 (top) by Steve Culpepper, courtesy of *Fine Homebuilding*, © The Taunton Press, Inc.; p. 44 (top right) by David Ericson, courtesy of *Fine Homebuilding*, © The Taunton Press, Inc.; pp. 44 (bottom right), 47 (right) McKie Roth Designs © Randy O'Rourke; p. 48 (left) © www.carolynbates.com; p. 61 (left) © www.davidduncanlivingston.com; p. 70 (bottom) © Ken Gutmaker

CHAPTER THREE: Walls, Ceilings, and Floors

pp. 73, 98 (bottom) by Steve Culpepper, courtesy of *Fine Homebuilding*, © The Taunton Press, Inc.; pp. 74 (bottom), 75, 78 (bottom), 79 (top), 83, 85 (right), 91, 96 (top), 101 (top), 102 © www.carolynbates.com; pp. 76 (top & bottom), 79 (bottom) © Grey Crawford; pp. 78 (top), 87 (bottom), 98 (top), 99 (top), 100 (top) © Joseph St. Pierre; pp. 80 (top), 92 (bottom) by David Ericson, courtesy of *Fine Homebuilding*, © The Taunton Press, Inc.; p. 85 (left) by Charles Miller, courtesy of *Fine Homebuilding*, © The Taunton Press, Inc.; pp. 94 (top), 95 courtesy The Sherwin-Williams Company; p. 99 (bottom) by Kevin Ireton, courtesy of *Fine Homebuilding*, © The Taunton Press, Inc.; pp. 103 (top), 104 (top & bottom right), 106 (top & bottom), 107 (bottom) courtesy Carlisle Wide Plank Floors, Stoddard, NH

CHAPTER FOUR: Kitchens, Baths, Storage, and Mudrooms

pp. 110, 117 (top & bottom), 123 (bottom) courtesy The Kennebec Company; p. 112 (bottom) by Steve Culpepper, courtesy of *Fine Homebuilding*, © The Taunton Press, Inc.; p. 113 courtesy Bluebell Kitchens, photo by Baruch Schwartz; pp. 115, 116 (top), 125 (bottom), 127 courtesy Crown Point Cabinetry; pp. 116 (bottom), 120 (top), 132, 134 (left) © www.davidduncanlivingston.com; p. 120 (bottom) © Joseph St. Pierre; pp. 123 (top, designed and built by Tom Hampson, Buffton, SC), 134 (right), 137 (left) © Brian Vanden Brink, Photographer 2004; p. 124 courtesy Gooseneck Designs, www.gooseneckdesigns.com, photo by Bill Schilling; pp. 125 (top), 139 (top & bottom) © Peter LaBau/The Classic Group, Inc.; p. 128 (bottom) courtesy Wood-Mode Fine Custom Cabinetry; pp. 129 (top), 152 (top), 153 (top), 157 (bottom) © Grey Crawford; p. 133 by Kevin Ireton, courtesy of *Fine Homebuilding*, © The Taunton Press, Inc.; p. 135 (left) by Scott Gibson, courtesy of *Fine Homebuilding*, © The Taunton Press, Inc.; pp. 135 (right), 141 (right) © Susan Kahn Photography; p. 137 (right) © Zachary Gaulkin; p. 138 (top) by Charles Miller, courtesy of *Fine Homebuilding*, © The Taunton Press, Inc.; p. 147 (top) © www.carolynbates.com

CHAPTER FIVE: Today's Classic Interior

pp. 166 (left), 169 (bottom) © Bruce Buck; p. 167 by Jefferson Kolle, courtesy of *Fine Homebuilding*, © The Taunton Press, Inc.; pp. 168, 170, 171 (top), 173 (left) © Joseph St. Pierre; p. 169 (top) by Steve Culpepper, courtesy of *Fine Homebuilding*, © The Taunton Press, Inc.; p. 174 (bottom) by Scott Gibson, courtesy of *Fine Homebuilding*, © The Taunton Press, Inc.; p. 174 (right) by Travis DuPont, Adams, MA, for Period Lighting Fixtures, Inc.; p. 175 (bottom) McKie Roth Designs © Randy O'Rourke; p. 176 (bottom left) courtesy Lighting by Hammerworks; pp. 176 (bottom right), 178 (top right), 179 (right) by Art Evans, Williamstown, MA, for Period Lighting Fixtures, Inc.; pp. 178 (top left), 179 (left) by Nick Whitman, Williamstown, MA, for Period Lighting Fixtures, Inc.; p. 180 (bottom right) by Period Lighting Fixtures, Inc.; p. 181 © www.carolynbates.com